Getting it

- A Behaviour C

Lesson Plans for Small Group Delivery
(Key Stages 3 and 4)

▸ As part of a pastoral support plan

▸ As a reintegration package following exclusion

▸ Within an in-school Behaviour Centre, Learning Support Unit or Pupil Referral Unit

Programme devised by:

Julie Casey,
Specialist Educational Psychologist (Behaviour)

Lucky Duck is more than a publishing house and training agency. George Robinson and Barbara Maines founded the company in the 1980s when they worked together as a head and psychologist developing innovative strategies to support challenging students.

They have an international reputation for their work on bullying, self-esteem, emotional literacy and many other subjects of interest to the world of education.

George and Barbara have set up a regular news-spot on the website. Twice yearly these items will be printed as a newsletter. If you would like to go on the mailing list to receive this then please contact us:

Lucky Duck Publishing Ltd. 3 Thorndale Mews, Clifton, Bristol, BS8 2HX, UK

Phone: 44 (0)117 973 2881   e-mail newsletter@luckyduck.co.uk

Fax: 44 (0)117 973 1707   website www.luckyduck.co.uk

ISBN 1 873 942 34 6

Published by Lucky Duck Publishing Ltd
3 Thorndale Mews, Clifton, Bristol BS8 2HX, UK

www.luckyduck.co.uk

Commissioned and Edited by George Robinson
Designed by Helen Weller
Illustrated by Tina Rae
Printed by Antony Rowe Limited

Reprinted November 2002, Revised format: December 2003

Getting it Right
- A Behaviour Curriculum

by

Julie Casey,
Specialist Educational Psychologist (Behaviour)

This resource was developed in close association with the Bristol Psychology Service.

With Thanks to:

Lesley Kaplan (Senior Educational Psychologist)

Jean Gross (Principal Educational Psychologist)

Sue May (Behaviour Manager, Hengrove School, Bristol)

Pauline Marson (Deputy Head, Henbury School, Bristol)

Shirley Stephenson and **Kate McKechnie** (St. George Community College, Bristol)

Eve Clarke (Behaviour Manager, Henbury School, Bristol)

Marilyn Coombes (Behaviour Co-ordinator, Brislington School, Bristol)

Brigid Allen (Excellence in Cities, Bristol)

Chris Lindup (Professional Trainer and Coach, Bristol)

Nikki Honeywell (Office Manager, East and Central Psychology Team, Bristol)

This book draws on, and complements the work of **Chris Wardle and Tina Rae** in the book entitled "*School Survival*" published by Lucky Duck Publishing Ltd, 2002.

How to use the CD-ROM

The CD-ROM contains a PDF file labelled 'Worksheets.pdf', which contains all the worksheets for each lesson in this resource. You will need Acrobat Reader version 3 or higher to view and print these resources.

The document is set up to print to A4 but you can enlarge the pages to A3 by increasing the output percentage at the point of printing using the page set-up settings for your printer.

To photocopy the worksheets directly from this book, set your photocopier to enlarge by 125% and align the edge of the page to be copied against the leading edge of the the copier glass (usually indicated by an arrow).

Contents

Introduction

Why do we need a 'Behaviour Curriculum'?

Over the past few years the government agendas for inclusion and for reducing exclusions and truancy have led to a greater awareness of the needs of pupils with Emotional and Behavioural Difficulties (EBD) in mainstream schools and lessons.

The appointment of Behaviour Co-ordinators within schools; and the setting up of Pupil Referral Units (PRUs), Learning Support Units (LSUs) under the Excellence in Cities initiative, within school Behaviour Centres, and the introduction of Pastoral Support Plans (PSPs) are just some of many responses that the government, LEAs and individual schools have made in an attempt to meet the needs of these pupils. In most cases integration into mainstream lessons is the aim.

Most forms of provision support designated pupils by withdrawing them from mainstream lessons and providing experiences and opportunities for them to identify, develop and practice the key skills they need to survive in the classroom in a small group, 'protected' environment and with time-limited intervention.

The 'Getting it Right' programme aims to provide these experiences and opportunities in a series of structured and comprehensive lesson plans for use with small groups at KS3 and 4.

As with any form of 'additional' or 'different' support, there will be an issue about priorities. If identified pupils are to be offered something 'different' to the majority of pupils (as with reading support), the time to do so has to come from somewhere. Many teachers believe that pupils with EBD are missing out on large amounts of learning because of their behaviour, and that teaching a behavioural curriculum for part of the day/week enables them to gain more than they lose. This will, however, need to be debated within individual schools.

Finally, it is important to be clear that the programme does not and cannot replace the need for a coherent whole-school framework for promoting positive behaviour. The need for school-wide policy, procedures and practices delivered consistently; explicit and agreed expectations; and the development of behaviour management skills for mainstream teachers' remain crucial to the achievement of all pupils, and none more so than those with EBD.

Who is it for?

Pupils are referred for small group behavioural support in a variety of contexts for a number of reasons:

- As part of a PSP
- For support at KS2/3 transfer
- As a result of cumulative sanctions (eg. removal from lessons because of their behaviour)
- Following fixed term exclusions (usually two or more)
- Because they are at risk of permanent exclusion
- Following permanent exclusion

Whatever the reason for their referral, these pupils will have difficulties in common. Many will lack the motivation to change their behaviour and the knowledge of how goals are set and achieved and most will lack self-belief and the key underlying skills of behavioural self-management. They are likely to have a restricted range of strategies for dealing with problematic situations and often resort to aggression. Many will find it difficult to 'survive' in the classroom because of their disorganisation, poor learning behaviours and difficult inter-personal interactions with staff and peers.

The 'Getting it Right' materials address all of these issues in a motivating, structured and comprehensive programme which aims to offer even the most troubled pupils the opportunity to develop the skills, knowledge, understanding and self-belief which will enable them to return to a mainstream curriculum, not as a 'model pupil' but as a 'survivor'.

The programme

Aims

The aims of the programme are:

- To help pupils develop the necessary motivation to want to change their behaviour
- To develop a positive mindset that will enable them to set and achieve goals
- To equip them with the skills and strategies to deal with common 'trigger' situations in the classroom
- To develop the ability to manage their feelings and develop the skills of anger control, assertiveness and conflict management

The Approach

The self-management approach used throughout the programme is based on cognitive-behavioural and solution-focused psychology, as these approaches have been shown to be the most effective in bringing about change. In addition, these approaches lead to greater transferability (from the group context to the classroom) as they do not depend as crucially on environmental conditions as do, for example, behaviourist approaches.

Content Outline

The programme consists of a series of lesson plans in four units. Each lesson plan includes: Learning objectives; Pupil organisation; Resources needed; Preparation required.

The first unit focuses on motivating pupils to want to change their behaviour. The second focuses on the importance of being able to set and achieve goals. The first two sessions teach the skills necessary to break down longer-term goals into more immediate and specific actions, and how to recognise and overcome obstacles. The third and fourth sessions focus on 'locus of control' (taking responsibility for our own behaviour) and a key strategy for goal attainment, positive thinking and self-talk.

Underlying successful behaviour change are certain key skills of emotional literacy. Principle among these are the ability to manage one's anger, assertiveness skills and the ability to manage conflict. These three key skills are the subject of Unit 3.

Unit 4 draws on all that has been learnt in the preceding units and focuses specifically on the classroom context, as this is where pupils must survive. An understanding of rules, rights and responsibilities is essential for classroom survival, and this is therefore dealt with first in the unit. The second session focuses in detail on what 'tools' or skills pupils will need in the classroom context, and sessions three and four focus on the trigger situations that most commonly cause conflict and confrontation in the classroom. The aim of these sessions is to widen the repertoire of strategies available to pupils and to consider the consequences of each choice in terms of the effect on their longer-term goals. The unit concludes with a session summing up the 'top ten' skills that constitute the 'survival mindset' and a 'model lesson' to practice all that has been learnt, in which their behaviour is assessed by an external adult. Pupils complete a self-assessment of their own progress.

General guidelines on setting up the programme

▸ **Group composition.** Plan the composition of the group carefully, avoiding pupil pairings that are likely to 'sabotage' the course aims. Where possible, include a range of ages (usually within a key stage) and balance gender, ethnicity and 'severity of need'. In general, a ratio of five pupils to one teacher seems to work most effectively. The programme can be delivered by a teacher or by another adult employed by the school - the crucial factor in the success of the programme is likely to be the quality of the relationship between the adult and pupils.

▸ **Session length.** Session length will be dictated by the constraints and opportunities operating in individual schools. Session plans provide enough material for a notional 50 minute session, but teachers can vary lesson length by selecting from the activities outlined, or by developing a theme perceived as useful and supplementing the session with other materials/activities.

- **Required resources.** Masters for all worksheets and overhead transparencies are supplied. Resources required are listed at the beginning of each session. For most sessions, an overhead projector, flip-chart, marker pens and general pupil resources (paper, felt-pens etc.) are all that is required. However, optional resources are suggested for several sessions, including the use of a video recorder and play-back facility - a resource which does much to motivate and which has proved extremely effective in 'getting the message across' to pupils in an immediate and relevant way.

- **Organisation.** ('difference' versus 'Consistency'). Ensure that lessons can take place at the agreed time in a comfortable area where disruptions will be minimised. Pupils often appreciate refreshments (check dietary requirements with parents) and respond well to special privileges (such as comfortable chairs, 'posh' files). A degree of 'difference' to normal lessons is usually helpful in breaking learnt negative responses to classroom situations, but needs to be balanced by the clear understanding that whole-school expectations operate throughout, as this is the context to which pupils must return.

- **Parental involvement.** This is crucial. Send a letter to parents explaining what the course is for and asking for their co-operation. Ideally parents should be given the opportunity to meet with staff and talk about the course aims and content. This provides an opportunity to establish a positive relationship with parents and discuss how the lessons can be reinforced at home. Regular contact should be kept up with parents throughout the course, perhaps with a positive letter being sent home weekly.

- **The role of mainstream teachers.** The effectiveness of the lessons learnt in the group depends fundamentally on the co-operation of the pupils' mainstream teachers. They need to know what is being taught and their role in reinforcing the aims of the sessions. This, along with potential sources of resentment and irritation, need to be addressed at a whole school level (eg. pupils being withdrawn from their classes, being perceived as getting 'treats for being naughty' and so on). When pupils are withdrawn from subject lessons, 'catch-up' arrangements will need to be agreed.

- **Whole school framework.** The programme is designed to support individuals with additional needs, and should be seen as complimentary and additional to the whole school framework for teaching positive behaviour. When pupils are reintegrated into mainstream lessons, teachers will need to have strategies for welcoming them back and ensuring that their own practice supports positive behaviour choices. Arrangements for reintegration will need to be agreed at the whole school level in order to ensure the necessary degree of consistency and commitment.

- **Individual 'interviews' with group members.** It is wise to see pupils individually before bringing them together as a group. The first session is designed to be delivered on a one to one basis, in order to enable the teacher to begin to build a personal relationship with the pupil, and establish commitment to the course and the overall behavioural expectations.

General guidelines on delivering the programme

Pupils with EBD respond, as all pupils do, to good teaching. Where they often differ from those pupils who cope without support is in their response to poor teaching, or a lack of preparation or organisation. The delivery of the sessions therefore needs to represent the very best practice. This will include: thorough preparation with tasks well differentiated according to the needs of the individuals; clear learning objectives made explicit to pupils; resources prepared and to hand; a clear structure to the lesson; a well-paced balance of activities; and, finally, a stimulating and enthusiastic style of presentation.

Although important for all pupils, the following additional factors have proved to be particularly significant in the successful delivery of group work to pupils with EBD:

▶ **The relationship between pupils and teacher.** Pupils with EBD often have a greater need to know that they are accepted and valued as individuals, as well as an exaggerated response to negative labelling and put-downs (usually as a result of their history). Pupils with EBD have often lost trust in teachers and built up negative patterns of interaction with authority figures. The specialist teacher needs to be able to build up a relationship of trust with pupils, and to engage with the effective side of pupils in a way that consistently builds self-esteem. The building of this relationship will take place over time, as the teacher demonstrates that he or she will do as they say they will do; accepts pupils back after setbacks with a 'clean slate'; and demonstrates his or her respect for, and valuing of, pupils as individuals (even when initially it is not reciprocated).

▶ **Clarity of expectations and rules.** With EBD pupils, it is important to gain explicit commitment to these within the group. This will be more easily gained if pupils are able to contribute to their formulation. It is important however, that these fall within the school's overall discipline policy and are not significantly 'different' to other classes. Many teachers of pupils with EBD use the concept of pupils 'working towards' a particular expectation with a time-limited differentiation of consequence, in recognition of the fact that behaviour change takes time. Group sessions provide an ideal opportunity to make explicit points and discuss school rules, as well as developing strategies for supporting pupils in keeping to them. Some sample groundrules are suggested in the section entitled 'The development of learning behaviours through programme activities', and school rules are explicitly dealt with in Unit 4.

▶ **The consistent and fair use of motivational systems.** Pupils with EBD often require more external motivation, as they have yet to develop internal motivational systems (which requires the ability to delay gratification) and have learnt that many academic tasks are not intrinsically motivating. They tend to need more immediate positive reinforcement and more consistency and 'following through'. In addition, many EBD pupils perceive themselves to have been unfairly treated and are hypersensitive to any 'injustice'. Motivational systems therefore need to be developed with these points in mind. Teachers have found it useful to supplement the school's standard reward system with additional devices (such as points leading to a cumulative group 'reward', letters home, raffles with small session by session prizes etc.).

▶ **The consistent and fair use of agreed sanction systems.** Pupils will often feel that they have been unfairly sanctioned by teachers in the past, so it is important to make explicit what will happen within the group if unacceptable behaviours occur, and why (the rights of others, the importance of learning etc.). This will involve being explicit about what constitutes unacceptable behaviour, and the group should be involved in discussions about this (although the teacher will need to ensure that the overall school rules are made explicit). Some teachers have found it useful to use a staged approach which is made explicit to pupils and displayed. An example of a staged approach used successfully by teachers is:

- ▸ Low level intervention
- ▸ Rule reminder
- ▸ 'Yellow card'- warning
- ▸ 'Red card' - two minutes time out of the group but within the room
- ▸ School sanction - e.g. detention
- ▸ Exit from classroom with follow up

▸ **The explicit teaching of routines and 'learning behaviours'.** The content of the programme is designed to mirror the sorts of learning tasks generally required in mainstream classrooms. These include:

- ▸ Listening to the teacher
- ▸ Answering and asking questions
- ▸ Group discussions
- ▸ Group/pair activities
- ▸ Individual activities
- ▸ Group games

It is suggested that in addition to the 'content' of the course, teachers pay particular attention to the development of the process skills that pupils will need in the classroom (the 'how' as well as the 'what'), using the activities provided to do so. The activities provide the opportunity to make explicit, model and teach the learning behaviours required for these 'classroom tasks'. In the next section some sample 'learning behaviours' are outlined for these different tasks. These can be introduced to pupils as the activities demand, and reinforced as the programme progresses.

The development of learning behaviours through programme activities

Many learning behaviours are common to all types of activity. These represent the framework for all work that goes on in the sessions and will need to be made explicit, discussed and displayed as 'Ground rules'. It is important that pupils contribute to their formulation, in order to ensure a sense of ownership and increase the chances of commitment to them. Sample ground rules and learning behaviours are listed below.

Groundrules

- 'Classroom talk' at all times (e.g. no swearing or inappropriate language/forms of address)
- Mobile phones switched off
- Respect others (e.g. no put-downs, racism or sexism)
- Ask permission to leave your seat
- Keep the noise level acceptable
- Do your best
- Keep your focus on the task or topic in hand

Listening to the teacher/asking and answering questions

- Listen (looking at the teacher and sitting still)
- Think about what is being said
- Put your hand up if you do not understand or want to answer a question (don't call out)
- Be prepared to wait a short while

Group discussions

- Show that you have something to say (don't call out)
- Speak one at a time - listen to others
- Let everyone have their first say before you have your second
- Disagree without being disagreeable

Group/pair activity/game

- Listen carefully to the instructions or rules
- Ask if you are not sure what to do
- Make sure you have everything you need for the task
- Decide together who will do what
- Share materials fairly - wait sensibly to use something that someone else is using
- Treat materials with respect - put them away in the correct places
- Be patient - wait for your turn

Individual work

- Do it on your own - don't let others distract you from the task
- Use the school rules for setting out work (date, name, title etc.)
- Start quickly, keep at it and do your best!

Reintegration and follow-up

The method of reintegrating pupils back into mainstream lessons will vary according to the particular set up within the organisation of the provision in which the programme has been delivered. Some pupils will have been attending most of their mainstream lessons over the entire duration of the programme, some will have been withdrawn completely for a period of weeks, and others will be somewhere along this continuum. The following model therefore represents an 'ideal' method of reintegrating pupils into a lesson, the principles of which could be adapted to fit the individual contexts of schools and other educational provisions.

The principle behind the model is that of offering pupils 'scaffolding' to support their reintegration, which can be dismantled piece by piece as progress is made. The support available is therefore intensive to begin with, and decreases until it is removed altogether. Some pupils may of course not reach the stage of full mainstream integration with no support, and individual plans will need to be made for these pupils to support their continued inclusion in mainstream classes.

The following steps are suggested:

- The final session of Unit 4 allows the group to experience a model lesson, delivered by the group teacher, with a mainstream member of staff observing.

- Following this session, the teacher may decide to offer a further group session, this time led by a mainstream teacher, with themselves as observer and with feedback offered to the group or individuals. This could include selected 'role-model' pupils from the mainstream group that the pupils will be returning to.

- Pre-integration strategies should be put in place with individual teachers, to whom pupils will be returning. Strategies that increase the chances of successful reintegration include meetings set up between individuals and the teachers concerned, where the teacher is able to discuss the pupils needs and progress with them, and so begin to build a positive relationship. Care must be taken that this meeting does not become a negative, 'rule laying-down' session dominated by teacher demands (whole school policy and discussion will be crucial in determining attitudes here). Pupils should be given the chance to 'catch up' with work that has been covered during their absence from class, and to talk through the work that the class will be covering when the child returns. Teachers may need support in planning strategies for welcoming back the student, for recognising efforts made and for focusing on the pupil's individual targets. This could take place in a meeting between the group and subject teachers.

- Supported reintegration to mainstream lessons now takes place. It is suggested that pupils reintegrate into one or two subject areas at a time, beginning with those in which success is most likely. It is helpful if a known adult (perhaps a teaching assistant) can be placed within the classroom to support the pupil, reminding him or her of targets and strategies. The assistant can provide monitoring which can be used to allocate previously agreed rewards, when targets are achieved.

- The next step is for teaching assistant support to be withdrawn from lessons where progress is good. Monitoring passes at this stage to the subject-teacher (and pupil), who agrees with the pupil what will be monitored, when and how. The reward structure should remain in place, and the pupil may be allocated a regular support 'slot' with a favoured worker, or a 'bolt-card' which enables them to use the behaviour base at times of particular difficulty.

▶ The final stage of the reintegration process is when specialist support has been withdrawn from all lessons (although teaching assistants attached to particular lessons can continue to be used to support the pupil), and a final review suggests that the pupil no longer requires monitoring.

A diagrammatic representation of the process from beginning to end is shown on the next page:

Model of achieving re-integration

Motivation to change behaviour:

(UNIT 1)

▶ Wanting to avoid exclusion
▶ Having a long-term vision

Understanding goal setting and skills needed to achieve goals:

(UNIT 2)

▶ Target setting
▶ Overcoming obstacles
▶ Developing an internal 'locus of control'
▶ Positive thinking and self-talk

Learning key underlying skills

(UNIT 3)

▶ Managing feelings
▶ Assertiveness
▶ Solving problems and

Identifying and practising key 'classroom survival skills' and strategies **(UNIT 4)**

Putting it all together **(UNIT 4 and FOLLOW UP)**

▶ Group lesson with EBD teacher, mainstreem teacher observing
▶ Group lesson with mainstream teacher, EBD teacher observing
▶ Pre-lesson integration strategies (meeting teacher/catch up work etc.)
▶ Supported reintegration with monitoring and rewards (increasing range of lessons)
▶ Unsupported reintegration with monitoring and rewards (increasing range)
▶ Full-time mainstream. Support ends.

Unit 1

Why Should I Change My Behaviour?

1.1 'So what if I'm excluded'

(preparatory one to one session)

1.2 A vision for the future -

identifying positive and negative outcomes

Lesson Planning Sheet

Unit 1   **Why Should I Change My Behaviour?**

Session 1   **'So what if I'm excluded?'**

Note: This session is an individual one to one session

Learning objectives:

- ▸ Gaining commitment from the pupil to attend the course
- ▸ Understanding the effects of exclusion on life-chances
- ▸ Establishing base-line for commitment to changing behaviour and confidence in ability to do so

Pupil organisation:

- ▸ One to one session with teacher

Resources needed:

- ▸ 1 copy for each pupil of worksheets 1.1, 1.2, 1.3
- ▸ Individual file for pupil's work

Preparation:

Ensure that you are familiar with the course content (to be able to give a synopsis to the pupil).

Ensure correct information regarding dates, times, location etc. is available.

Find out the relevant statistics and procedures operating within the school regarding exclusion, (for Activity 3).

Lesson Plan 1.1

This first lesson should ideally take place on a one-to-one basis in order to attain the individual's commitment to attend the programme, and to establish base-line measures without group dynamics influencing the results.

Activity 1 - Gaining commitment

Whether or not the programme is 'compulsory', the co-operation of the pupil is vital to the effectiveness of the group and to positive outcomes for the pupil. When introducing the course, its supportive function should be emphasised and factual information clearly given to the pupil (including dates, times, numbers and location, as well as an outline of the content of the course). An emphasis on the 'fun' elements of the course is usually effective in gaining commitment (particularly if video equipment is to be used) and work or displays from previous groups is often of interest. Confidence should be maintained that the programme will have a big impact on past behaviour patterns.

Motivational strategies (points, rewards, letters home etc.) can also be outlined at this point.

Activity 2 - Base-line assessment

Ask the pupil to complete **Worksheet 1.1** as honestly as they can, and explain that at the end of the course he or she will be asked to re-rate themselves in order to see how much progress they have made.

Activity 3 - Quiz: What do you know about exclusion?

A good 'warm-up' activity is to complete the quiz on **Worksheet 1.2**. The answers are given at the end of this lesson plan and can form the basis for a discussion about why the school does not want the pupil to be excluded, as well as allowing the teacher to gain an idea of the individual's level of understanding.

The teacher can then ask the pupil similar questions about what happens in their own school (pupils often do not really understand the exclusion procedures - many pupils who end up permanently excluded do not realise how 'close to the edge' they were). Information could include how many pupils were excluded; who decides about an exclusion; what the school will exclude pupils for; and the meaning of the various 'stages' of exclusion.

One of the most effective and credible ways of making exclusion a less attractive option for pupils is to organise a visit from a young person who was excluded and can 'tell it how it is' (but choose wisely…).

Activity 4 - 5 Good reasons not to get excluded

Ask the pupil to think of 5 reasons why it would not be good to get excluded (permanently) and ask him or her to record these on **Worksheet 1.3** (or act as the pupil's scribe). Discussion could focus on the positive effects of staying in school, the effect on families when exclusion occurs, the better life-chances of non-excluded pupils etc.

Activity 5 - Closing the deal!

Ask the pupil if they are prepared to give the programme a go. Accept any positive indication (a slightly raised eyebrow can be a breakthrough in terms of enthusiasm for some pupils). Remind the pupil of the motivational devices and clearly set out your own expectations of behaviour and any individual system of sanctions in operation.

Answers to Quiz:

2. 8,323

3. Age 13 (21%) and age 14 (26%)

4. 84 out of 100 are boys

5. No - only a small number return to mainstream school. Excluded pupils receive education at home, at a special school, or at a Pupil Referral Unit. Many do not get back into education for many months and never catch up

6. Very few go on to get any GCSEs
   ▸ They are more likely to be out of work at 18
   ▸ More likely to be homeless and use drugs
   ▸ More likely to become involved in crime
   ▸ More likely to end up going to prison

7. ▸ Verbal abuse to teachers
   ▸ Repeated general disruption
   ▸ Physical violence (usually when tempers are lost)

Base-line assessment

How do I rate my current behaviour in school?

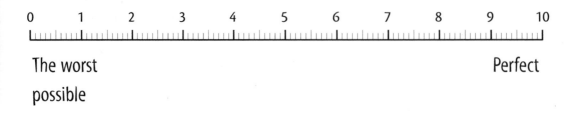

The worst
possible

Perfect

How much do I want to change my behaviour?

Not at all

A lot

How confident am I that I can change my behaviour and still be in
school in Y11?

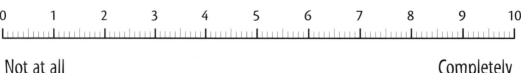

Not at all

Completely

How much do you know about exclusion?

▶ 1. What is the difference between 'fixed term' and 'permanent' exclusion?

▶ 2. How many pupils do you think were permanently excluded in England between 1999 and 2000?

▶ 3. At what age are most pupils excluded? Why do you think this is?

▶ 4. Do you think that more boys or more girls were excluded? Why?

▶ 5. Do most excluded pupils go back into mainstream school? Where do they go?

▶ 6. What sort of lives do you think people who were excluded from school have?

▶ 7. What are the main reasons for exclusion?

Five good reasons not to get excluded

1. _____

2. _____

3. _____

4. _____

5 _____

Lesson Planning Sheet

Unit 1   **Why should I change my behaviour?**

Session 2   **A vision for the future - identifying and negative outcomes**

Note: This is the first group-work session

Learning objectives:

- ▸ Developing a positive long-term 'vision'
- ▸ Identifying helping and hindering factors in achieving it

Pupil organisation:

- ▸ Group discussion
- ▸ Individual activity

Resources needed:

- ▸ 1 copy of worksheets 1.5, 1.7 (blown up to A3 or as an OHT if possible)
- ▸ Copies of worksheets 1.4, 1.5, 1.6 for each pupil
- ▸ Flip-chart/whiteboard and marker
- ▸ Materials for pupils to draw pictures

Preparation:

Rules and expectations on display to refer to.

Lesson Plan 1.2

Welcome pupils. Introduce and discuss ground rules and expectations of working behaviour (as discussed in initial individual sessions). Recap on reward and sanction systems.

Activity 1 - Best and worst outcomes

Write the words BEST OUTCOME and WORST OUTCOME on the flip-chart. Ask pupils to imagine the best life they can think of having when they are 25. Get each of them to describe in turn what their life will be like. Prompt with headings such as job, car, type of house, where they will be living, what they will be doing in their spare time, clothes they will be wearing, what their family will be saying about them to friends etc. Record their ideas under the heading 'Best outcome' on the flipchart.

Then ask them to imagine the worst life they can think of having at 25 (or think of someone they would least like to be like). Encourage them to think what it would be like, eg. no job, no money, no home, in prison, no friends, horrible clothes, feeling bad about themselves, family not talking to them etc.. Record these under the heading 'Worst Outcome'.

Ask which is the 'positive outcome' and which is the 'negative outcome'. Explain these terms if necessary. Ask pupils who would like to achieve the first set of goals and who would like to achieve the second.

Ask pupils to record their own personal 'Best' and 'Worst Outcomes' on **Worksheet 1.4**.

Finish the activity by reading the motivational quotation on **Worksheet 1.5** and asking pupils to write in their own dream in a sentence or two.

'Just as you don't just get in a car and drive without knowing the destination, you can't live your life to the full without knowing where you're heading. Everybody needs a dream…'

Activity 2 - What can help or hinder me in achieving my dream?

Give out **Worksheet 1.6** and ask pupils to say in turn one thing that will help them achieve their goal, and one thing that may get in the way. Use **Worksheet 1.7** as a reference list, or if the pupils are stuck for ideas.

After the group discussion, ask pupils to complete **Worksheet 1.6** for themselves, supporting them as necessary.

Activity 3 - Ideas for establishing the 'vision'

▸ Get pupils to draw themselves and their 'ideal future'. Ensure that pupils keep this work in their individual folders or display finished work.

▸ Ask pupils to imagine that they have finished school as successful pupils and achieved their own dream. Tell them that you are going to 'interview' them as if they were 25 year olds, asking them how they managed to become so successful and achieve their dreams. Ask them to answer 'in role' and prepare some questions for them to respond to. Pupils may not feel comfortable talking in front of other group members at this stage of the programme, so it is best to do this activity with those who volunteer. Begin with easy questions (requiring short, factual answers) and moving on to more open-ended prompts. Reward any contributions. Early questions could include: what is your name? How old are you? What is your job now? How much do you earn? Did you have to get qualifications at school to do this job? The focus could then move on to asking pupils how they managed to do well at school when so many pupils get excluded, e.g. how did you manage to keep out of trouble? Did other pupils ever try to get you into trouble and how did you handle this? Did teachers ever get on your nerves and if so how did you manage not to get sent out of lessons? What did you do when you found the work difficult? The interview could finish with asking the pupil what advice they would give to a pupil at school now who was close to exclusion/returning from exclusion.

Worksheet 1.4

Best Possible Outcome (Positive)	Worst Possible Outcome (Negative)

Thought for the day…

"Just as you don't just get in a car and drive without knowing the destination, you can't live your life to the full without knowing where you're heading. Everybody needs a dream…"

My dream

_____

_____

_____

_____

What will help me or hinder me in achieving my dream?

Things that will help me	Things that will hinder me

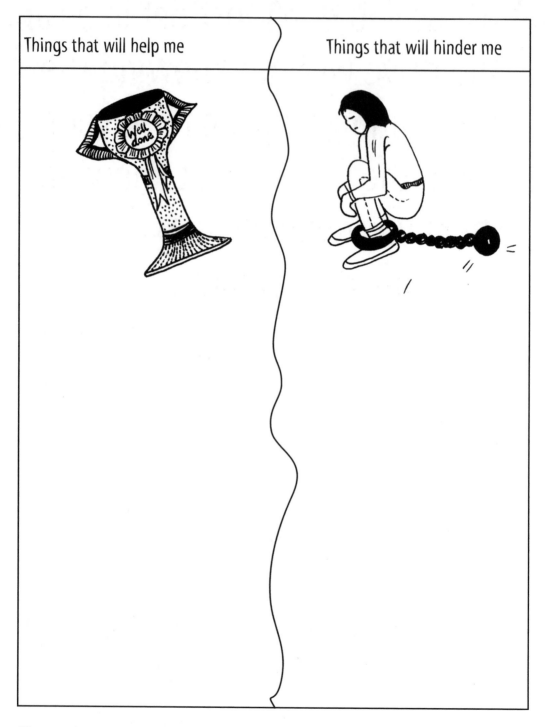

Helping and hindering factors

Other people

- Friends who persuade me to do the wrong thing
- My parents will support me
- Particular teachers who like me
- Other people in my life who support me
- Teachers who don't like me

Personal qualities

- I am good at sticking at things
- I am good at earning money
- I do not always do what I say I am going to do
- I give up easily
- I am popular with other people
- I lose my temper too much
- I am brave
- I am reliable
- I do not always think about what I say

Skills and knowledge

- I know something about the job I want to do
- I can do............... already
- I don't know anything about it yet
- My parents/teachers/others know a lot about ...
- I am good at.........
- I am not so good at........

Unit 2

Achieving Goals

2.1 One step at a time

2.2 Recognising and overcoming obstacles

2.3 Taking responsibility

2.4 Positive thinking and self-talk

Lesson Planning Sheet

Unit 2 **Achieving Goals**

Session 1 **One step at a time**

Learning objectives:

▸ Knowing what a goal is

▸ Understanding how goals are achieved one step at a time

▸ Setting a target to help achieve a goal

Pupil organisation:

▸ Group discussion

▸ Individual or paired activity

Resources needed:

▸ 1 copy of worksheets 2.1, 2.3, 2.5 (blown up to A3 or as OHT if possible)

▸ 1 copy per pupil of worksheets 2.2, 2.4, 2.6, 2.7

▸ Flip-chart/whiteboard and marker pen

▸ Scissors and glue

Preparation:

(Optional) Pictures of famous people who might be admired by pupils could be collected as a source of motivation for Activity 1.

Lesson Plan 2.1

Activity 1 - What is a goal?

Get the group to list people they admire for what they can do eg. famous footballers/film stars/singers. What have those people done or achieved that they admire?

Ask the question, 'what is a goal?'. Draw out the point that it is essentially 'something you want to do but can't, but you work at it, and eventually you can'.

Ask what goals they themselves have achieved. Use **Worksheet 2.1**. Can they add one other goal each to the list?

Activity 2 - Is it easy to achieve a goal?

Ask pupils to write a goal they have achieved on **Worksheet 2.2**, then question pupils on their achievement using the questions on the worksheet. If they are not forthcoming, use an example of your own (a skill that you have learnt) or ask one of the pupils to pretend to be one of the people they admire and answer the questions from their point of view.

Finish the activity with the quote on **Worksheet 2.3** and discuss what it means.

Activity 3 - What do you need to do to achieve your goal?

Discuss with pupils what they need to do to achieve a goal. Use **Worksheet 2.4** as a summary and talk about the Michael Jordan quotes on the importance of a vision and on failure. Relate to the pupils own 'vision' of their preferred future, outlined in previous sessions.

Activity 4 - Breaking down the big picture into little goals and setting a goal

Worksheet 2.5 can be used to introduce this activity, which emphasises the need to DO something as a first step to achieve a goal.

What are the little steps to achieve the bright future? Pupils discuss what smaller goals they need to achieve before they get to the future they have outlined for themselves.

Use **Worksheets 2.6** and **2.7** as a model for the process of breaking down a big goal into a series of little goals by working backwards.

Introduce **Worksheet 2.6** and talk pupils through the left-hand column, starting at the top. The top box represents the 'longest-term' goal ('my goal for one year after I leave school'), the next one down represents the goal that would have to be achieved to attain the goal above, and so on.

The task for pupils is to 'match up' the goals listed on **Worksheet 2.7** to the correct 'time-frame' box on Worksheet 2.6. Ask pupils 'Which goal on Worksheet 2.7 matches the top box on **Worksheet 2.6** 'My goal for one year after I leave school'?' The goal that fits this time-frame is 'Have a good job with a high salary so that I can save to buy what I want...'. Ask pupils which goals they would have had to achieve in order to get this good job on the day they leave school (second timeframe down). Help them to identify the goal ('get good exam grades; have a good reference and attendance record'). Repeat for the other goals listed for the 'next few years' and 'next three months' timeframes.

The key learning point is that goals become more specific as they become more immediate. The question for pupils to ask themselves is 'What would have to happen before I could achieve this goal?' and then to be as precise as possible.

Finally, ask pupils to complete their own goal for next week. Pupils often need support in setting small goals. Help them by asking them what specifically they would have to do in order to achieve the goals they have matched up for the 'next three months' timeframe. What would the teacher see them doing? For example, in order to 'stay in lessons', they would need to do specific things, such as not shout out, stay in their seat, tell the teacher politely if they are not happy with something etc.

What is a goal?

- Playing for Manchester United
- Giving up smoking
- Writing your name
- Running the London Marathon
- Riding a bike
- Climbing Mount Everest
- Competing in the Olympic Games
- Getting 5 GCSEs
- Staying in a French lesson
- Owning a BMW
- Becoming a doctor
- Learning to do addition

What goal have you achieved?

How did you achieve your goal?

The goal that I have achieved.

_____

_____

Could you do it straight away?

How did you get to be able to do it?

Did you learn it all at once, or a little bit at a time?

Was it ever hard?

Did you ever feel that you didn't want to practice?

Did you ever feel that you wouldn't be able to do it?

Did you ever want to give up?

How did it feel when you could do it or when
you achieved what you had set out to do?

Doing something difficult

"The things in life that are worth doing
are often the most difficult. But that's
because they're worth it. The more
difficult you find something, the more
valuable it will be when you achieve it."

How do people achieve their goals?

"I don't sweat for three hours a day just to know what it feels like to sweat!" Michael Jordan, with an eye on the long term

- ▶ They have a vision - they know where they want to be
- ▶ They take one step at a time
- ▶ They believe they can do it
- ▶ They know that what they do is up to them - they don't make excuses
- ▶ They tell themselves they can do it
- ▶ They keep the long-term goal in mind
- ▶ They keep going - even when it's hard
- ▶ They practice, practice and then practice some more
- ▶ They know they will fail sometimes, but they keep going anyway

"I've missed more than 9,000 shots in my career. I've lost almost 300 games. Twenty-six times I've been trusted to take the game-winning shot and missed. I've failed over and over again in my life. And that is why I succeed."

Michael Jordan

Achieving your goal
- Taking one step at a time

Q: How do you eat an elephant?

A: One bite at a time.

When you cycle up a long, steep hill, don't look at the top. Keep your eyes on the yard or so in front of you - it will look flat and you'll be amazed at how quickly you reach the top.

Steps to my fantastic future

My
Fantastic
Future

My goal for one year after I have left school	
My goal for the day I leave school	
My goal for the next few years	
My goal for the next three months	

My goal for next week (one thing I am going to do to help me stay in lessons)
Write your own goal here

Match up the goals with the time-frames

▶ Take away good exam grades

▶ Have a good reference and attendance record

▶ Set and achieve behaviour targets

▶ Go to agreed lessons

▶ Stay in lessons

▶ Get a good job and earn a decent salary so that I can save to buy what I want…

▶ Go to all lessons and complete work

▶ Control behaviour so that I don't get into trouble

Lesson Planning Sheet

Unit 2   **Achieving Goals**

Session 2 **Recognising and overcoming obstacles**

Learning objectives:

▸ Recognising and being prepared for the obstacles that can hinder the achievement of goals

▸ Becoming conscious of when excuses are used and recognising the effect of these excuses

▸ Understanding the skills and qualities necessary for successful goal achievement

Pupil organisation:

▸ Group discussion

▸ Group game

▸ Group activity

▸ Individual activity

Resources needed:

▸ 1 copy of worksheet 2.13 (blown up to A3 or as an OHT if possible)

▸ 1 copy per pupil of worksheet 2.8, 2.9, 2.10, 2.12

▸ Prepared cards made from worksheet 2.11

▸ Flip-chart/whiteboard and marker pen

▸ Materials for making an 'Excuses' book

▸ Materials for making a poster (optional)

Preparation:

Prepare worksheet 2.11 as indicated in Activity 4.

Lesson Plan 2.2

Activity 1 - How did it go?

Recap on the goals pupils set for the week. Ask for feedback on how they did, what went well and what did not go so well. Praise any success and ask pupils for reasons why it was not possible to achieve their target all the time. Note these reasons on the flip-chart.

Reiterate the fact that it is DIFFICULT to achieve a goal. Remind pupils of **Worksheet 2.3** ('Doing something Difficult'). Talk about the obstacles to achieving a goal - most 'reasons' will fall into one of these categories:

- Not believing you are in control - it's not your fault
- Not believing in yourself - thinking the task is too hard
- Not keeping at it - giving up at the first hurdle
- Forgetting your long-term goal for the pleasure of the moment
- Peer pressure - caring what friends think/wanting to impress friends.

Activity 2 - Which obstacles get in my way?

Give out **Worksheet 2.8** and explain that during the coming sessions, they will be working on overcoming these obstacles so that they can achieve their goals. Let pupils categorise 'excuses' using the 'giving up smoking' examples on **Worksheet 2.9**. Which sort of obstacle is standing in the way of the person who wants to give up smoking when they say each of the excuses to themselves? Then repeat the exercise using **Worksheet 2.10** ('Excuses for getting into trouble in lessons').

Ask pupils to think about which 'obstacle' gets in their way as they try to achieve their target in lessons during the coming days.

Activity 3 - Make an 'Excuses Book'

A fun activity is to make a 'book of excuses' and ask for all the excuses pupils use when they get into trouble in school. These can be numbered and written into the book. This book can then be added to at any time, and when excuses are used, a reference to the book (humorously delivered where appropriate) can be useful in helping pupils to begin to recognise their own patterns of behaviour.

The serious underlying point to be made here is that, at the end of the day, excuses are just that - they do not help pupils achieve their positive outcomes.

You may like to get the group to think of a short sharp saying or question to put on the cover of the book, such as 'Which are you? A buck passer or a buck earner?'.

Some teachers have taken the book and ceremoniously buried or burnt it to underline the point!

Activity 4 - People who succeed

Use **Worksheet 2.11 a-d** ('People who Succeed'). The statements should be cut up and stuck on individual cards, which are divided equally among the group. Each takes it in turn to start a sentence with the words 'People who succeed... 'finishing it with the statement written on the card. The player then has to decide if this is true or false, and other members of the group can agree or disagree, giving reasons as appropriate. The cards can be placed in two piles - 'true' and 'false'.

A poster for display could be made from the 'true' statements, if time is available.

Activity 5 - Planning to overcome obstacles

Use **Worksheet 2.12** to help pupils refine their plan for the coming week. The same goal or target or a different one can be selected. Discuss the headings on the planning sheet in terms of the obstacles they may encounter.

You could, if you chose, close the session using **Worksheet 2.13**:

"Four words that stand between you and success:

I
Can't
Be
Bothered"

Other useful motivational quotations to use to finish the session and 'call pupils to action' are:

"It's easy to know what to do - the difficulty lies in actually doing it".

"There are two reasons for failure - one is defeat, the other is giving up. Most failures are those who have just given up".

The five obstacles to achieving your goal

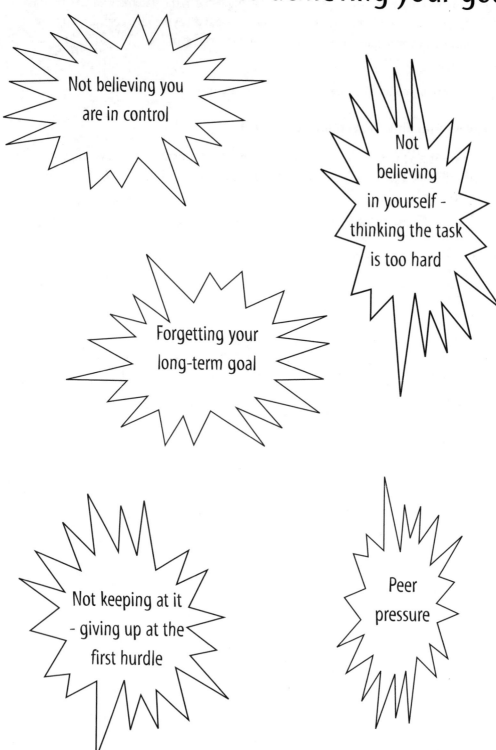

Not believing you are in control

Not believing in yourself - thinking the task is too hard

Forgetting your long-term goal

Not keeping at it - giving up at the first hurdle

Peer pressure

Which obstacle is in my way?

Excuses for not giving up smoking

I would have been able to give up but bad things kept happening - I had a row with my dad, my bike had a puncture so I was late and got into trouble at school.

I could do it if my friends didn't keep offering me cigarettes at break.

I can't go through the rest of my life without a cigarette - it's too hard to even think about it.

One won't hurt - I deserve that for giving up!

It's not my fault - cigarettes are addictive and if they sell them they can't expect people to be able to give up.

Which obstacle is in my way?

Excuses for getting into trouble in lessons

It wasn't my fault - it was boring and the teacher kept picking on me.

I've never been any good at science - there's no point trying because I'll never be able to do it anyway.

I'm already in trouble so there's no point going to French - I might as well bunk off.

They'll all think I've gone soft if I move just cos Miss X has told me too - I'm not looking like a keener.

It's more fun chucking paper - so what if I get into trouble? I don't like Mr. Y anyway.

People who succeed…

Have to be rich	Practise a lot
Are keeners	Work hard
Are born clever	Keep going even when the going gets tough

Go to posh schools	Put up with the boring bits
Are always popular	Accept failure and keep on anyway
Are just lucky	Believe they will be able to do it in the end

Find work easy

Don't make excuses

Blame other people when things go wrong

Know that it's down to them

Take responsibility

Have to be good looking

Tell themselves they can do it

Tell themselves they will never be able to do it

Keep their goal in mind

Don't have a goal

Have big houses

Break their goal down into smaller steps

Making a plan

What I want to achieve (my first step towards my goal)

_____

Why it would be a good thing to achieve

_____

Why I'm not doing it (my reasons and excuses)

_____

What will be hard about doing it

_____

What I can do differently to overcome the obstacles

_____

Planning for the obstacles

Four words that stand between you and success:

I
can't
be
bothered

Lesson Planning Sheet

Unit 2   **Achieving Goals**

Session 3 **Taking responsibility**

Learning objectives:

▸ Developing an internal locus of control

▸ Believing that behaviour change is possible

Pupil organisation:

▸ Group discussion

▸ Group game

▸ Individual or pair activity

Resources needed:

▸ 1 copy of worksheet 2.14 (blown up to A3 or as an OHT if possible)

▸ 1 copy of worksheet 2.15 (A3 or A4)

▸ 1 copy per pupil of worksheet 2.18

▸ Prepared cards made from worksheets 2.16 and 2.17

▸ Flip-chart/whiteboard and marker

Preparation:

Prepare worksheets 2.16 and 2.17 as indicated in Activity 2.

Lesson Plan 2.3

Activity 1 - introducing the idea of 'locus of control'

Show pupils **Worksheet 2.14** which shows the following quotation:

"A lot of growing up takes place between 'it fell' and 'I dropped it".

Discuss what this means. The following explanation can be used for introducing the idea of 'locus of control'.

Some people never take any responsibility for their behaviour. Whether it's getting into trouble for swearing at another pupil, playing badly in a football match, or not doing well in a subject at school, they will always put it down to something outside themselves - it's the other pupil's fault for winding them up, the teacher's fault for being boring, the coach for shouting at the wrong time, the weather - anything rather than them.

Some people never take any credit for what they do well. When they do do something well they will often put it down to luck, or to the other team being rubbish, or the test being easy.

The truth is that we always have a choice - we are responsible for the way we choose to behave, how hard we work, how much effort we put in to practising a sport. Luck sometimes plays a part (you might win the lottery), but usually what happens to us is a result of our own choices. If we believe that we are responsible (for good and bad things) we have 'internal control' (or poshly 'an internal locus of control'). If we believe that things outside of ourselves are always responsible for our success or failure, then we have 'external control' (or 'an external locus of control').

Activity 2 - Locus of control

Prepare **Worksheets 2.16** and **2.17** by cutting out each statement and sticking it on to an individual card.

Place **Worksheet 2.15** on the table - 'internal' and 'external' locus of control . Give out or read out cards and ask pupils to place them, in turn, in the correct box: 'internal' or 'external'.

Activity 3 - Discovering pupils' own 'locus of control'

Remind pupils about their own achievements, discussed in previous sessions. Ask them for the reasons they think they did well. Record these on the flip chart. Ask the others to say whether the pupil is showing an 'internal' or 'external' locus of control. (Be prepared with some examples of your own - pupils may be reticent about talking about their achievements).

Ask the question: Which is more helpful - an internal or external locus of control? And which helps you to do better next time?

Draw out the point that an internal locus of control means that you always have a choice. You can work towards a positive or a negative outcome.

Example: A pupil swears at a teacher. The teacher could choose to swear back at the pupil or control his or her anger and use the school discipline system to deal with it. What would be the positive or negative outcome for the teacher of each of these courses of action?

Activity 4 - Ten little words with a mighty meaning

Give out **Worksheet 2.18** and ask pupils (individually or in pairs) to rearrange the words to make a sentence about taking responsibility. A clue is that the first word has a capital letter!

(Answer: If it is to be, it is up to me)

Activity 5 - Putting it into practice

Ask pupils to think about their own choices at any 'critical moment' during their day at school. Remind them to say 'I have a choice' to themselves and to choose the behaviours that will lead them to a positive outcome.

Taking responsibility

A lot of growing up takes place between 'it fell' and 'I dropped it'...

Internal Locus of Control

External Locus of Control

I mucked around in class because the teacher was boring.

I did really well in that maths test because I've worked hard over the past few weeks.

I did well in that spelling test because it was so easy.

I didn't play well today because I've missed the last two practices.

I know what I did was wrong but it wasn't my fault. They made me do it.

I can't do anything right because the teacher doesn't like me.

I scored because we worked really well as a team today.

I didn't get into trouble today because I stopped myself from answering back.

My report was better this year - the teachers are much nicer.

I don't usually beat Curtis - he must have been off form today.

I've got a lucky charm and whenever I have it in my pocket I seem to do well.

I crashed into him because I was thinking about something else and wasn't really paying much attention.

It was really hard to qualify for the under 16s, but all that training paid off.

I got selected for the under 16s because the others were no good.

Everybody was doing it but I got into trouble because I decided to go along with the crowd.

Ten little words with a mighty meaning

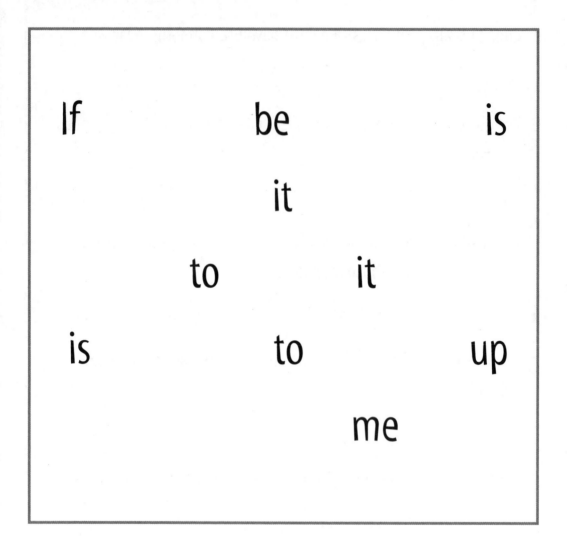

Rearrange these words to make a sentence about taking responsibility.

Lesson Planning Sheet

Unit 2   **Achieving Goals**

Session 4   **Positive thinking and self-talk**

Learning objectives:

‣ Understanding the links between our thoughts and our behaviour

‣ Using positive self-talk to change behaviour patterns

Pupil organisation:

‣ Group activity

‣ Group discussion

‣ Group game

‣ Individual, pair or group activity

Resources needed:

‣ 1 copy of worksheets 2.20, 2.21, 2.22 (blown up to A3 or as an OHP if possible)

‣ 1 copy per pupil of worksheet 2.23

‣ Prepared cards made from worksheet 2.19

‣ Prepared cards and game base-boards made from worksheets 2.24, 2.25 a-d

‣ Flip-chart/whiteboard and marker pen

Preparation:

Prepare worksheet 2.19 as described in Activity 1.

Prepare cards and game base-boards from worksheets 2.24, 2.25 A-D as described in Activity 4.

Lesson Plan 2.4

Activity 1 - What you think affects your behaviour

Use **Worksheet 2.19** to make individual cards by cutting out the sentences (and sticking them on to card if they are to be re-used). Each card has a 'secrecy flap' which should be folded over to cover the words before giving the cards to the pupils. This is important as the pupils must not realise that they all have the same card.

Divide the group into two smaller groups. Give each pupil a card, ensuring that no-one can see anyone else's.

Tell the groups that their task is to find the 'f's (pronounce it 'effs') in their sentences. Tell one group that there are five 'f's on their cards, and the other that there are six. After 30 to 45 seconds ask them if they have found all of them, and then ask how many they found.

Although there are the same number of 'f's on each card, usually the '5' group' will find five and the '6's group, six. Tell them that there are in fact nine, and see if they can find all of them.

(This isn't as easy as it looks so I'll help you out here…

FINE **F**OOD IS THE OUTCOME O**F** YEARS O**F** LOCAL KNOWLEDGE WITH THE **F**OODSTU**FF**S **F**OUND IN THE AREA O**F** INTEREST).

The explanation to the difference can be explained as their thoughts influencing their actions. If you think there are only five to find then you stop looking for them.

Show **Worksheet 2.20** which gives two examples from the animal kingdom of 'thoughts' influencing behaviour (heard on television so I can't vouch for 100% accuracy!).

Activity 2 - 'If you think you can, or if you think you can't, you're right'

Remind pupils how you get good at something (recap on **Worksheet 2.4**, how people achieve their goals). One of the key success factors that helps people to keep going when things are tough is believing that they can do it.

Ask pupils to think of a time when they knew they could do something and when this belief helped them to keep going until they could. As usual, be ready with an example of your own.

Show **Worksheet 2.21** (the 'vicious circle' of believing you can't do something). What you think about yourself affects how hard you try.

If you don't try, you won't get better, and so your thought becomes true. Use the example on the worksheet to stimulate discussion of pupils' own experiences of this process.

Activity 3 - Changing the way you think to help you achieve success

Explain to pupils that we all have a running commentary going on in our heads all the time. The trouble is our brain thinks all our thoughts are true - it can't tell the difference between truth and lies, so we act on what we tell ourselves.

Show **Worksheet 2.22** to illustrate this. This describes the conscious and subconscious and how a lot of actions come from our sub-conscious (the 'hidden' and 'not very clever' part of our brain. It uses a comic-strip example to demonstrate the process. To illustrate this ask pupils if they have ever done anything and thought, 'Why did I do that?' or if there is anything they do that they don't have to think about - riding a bike for example.

Other examples of our conscious thoughts causing our subconscious to act in a way that is not in our interests are:

Thought (believed by sub-conscious)	Action (ordered by subconscious)
I can't control my anger - if he calls me a name I'll hit him, I know I will.	HIT HIM.
I'll never learn to read. Everyone in the world can do it except me. There's no point in trying.	THROW BOOK DOWN. REFUSE TO DO ANY WORK.

The key learning point is that it is only by changing what we choose to tell our subconscious, that we can change our actions.

Most of what we tell ourselves is not helpful. We are often our own worst enemy - some of the things we say to ourselves are WORSE than what our enemies would say. Ask for examples of negative things pupils tell themselves. Common ones are:

- ▶ I must be completely stupid to do that
- ▶ I can't control myself when I get angry
- ▶ I'll never be able to do that
- ▶ I'm no good at that…
- ▶ This is the most embarrassing thing that has ever happened to anybody
- ▶ I'll die if I have to sit here another moment

In psychology these are known as 'cognitive distortions' and include exaggerations and 'catastrophising'.

Ask them to think of a really good friend or older person who they believe would tell the truth about them. Would this person say these things were true?

We need to change the message that we give our sub-conscious. The good thing is that you don't have to believe the new messages - remember that the subconscious cannot tell the difference between truth and lies!

Give out **Worksheet 2.23** ('Changing the message'). For each thought listed ask pupils if it passes the 'good friend test' (i.e. would a good friend agree?), then re-phrase the thought so that it gives a positive message to the sub-conscious, as the example shows. This can be done as an individual, pair or group activity. Discuss what actions the negative and positive thoughts might lead to.

Activity 4 - The helpful thought game

For this game each pupil will need a game base-board. The base-board can be found on **Worksheet 2.24** which should be photocopied for each pupil. The sheet can be stuck on card and laminated for future use.

You will also need **Worksheets 2.25 a-d**, which contain the statements to be made into 'cards' which will be used in the game. Only one set of cards is needed. Cut out each statement and stick it onto an individual card.

Each pupil will need a counter.

Play the game by shuffling and distributing the cards equally among the players. Ask each player to read out their top card in turn (or read them out for the group in order to support the self-esteem of poorer readers). If the thought written on the card is helpful, the player moves one space along the track towards 'success'. If the thought is not helpful, the player moves one space backwards towards the 'exclusion' end of the track.

The winner is the pupil who reaches the final space first.

FINE FOOD IS THE OUTCOME OF YEARS OF LOCAL KNOWLEDGE WITH THE FOODSTUFFS FOUND IN THE AREA OF INTEREST	(Fold over secrecy flap to hide words)
FINE FOOD IS THE OUTCOME OF YEARS OF LOCAL KNOWLEDGE WITH THE FOODSTUFFS FOUND IN THE AREA OF INTEREST	(Fold over secrecy flap to hide words)
FINE FOOD IS THE OUTCOME OF YEARS OF LOCAL KNOWLEDGE WITH THE FOODSTUFFS FOUND IN THE AREA OF INTEREST	(Fold over secrecy flap to hide words)
FINE FOOD IS THE OUTCOME OF YEARS OF LOCAL KNOWLEDGE WITH THE FOODSTUFFS FOUND IN THE AREA OF INTEREST	(Fold over secrecy flap to hide words)
FINE FOOD IS THE OUTCOME OF YEARS OF LOCAL KNOWLEDGE WITH THE FOODSTUFFS FOUND IN THE AREA OF INTEREST	(Fold over secrecy flap to hide words)

You do what you think you can do!

If you keep flies in a jar with a cling-film top (with air holes and food) from birth until adulthood, they will never leave the jar, even when the cling-film top is removed!

If a baby elephant is tethered to a rope while it is growing up, it can only walk in a circle around the post to which it is tethered. If this rope is then removed, the elephant will not move outside this circle.

"If you think that you can, or if you think that you can't, you're right"

Success comes in 'cans'. Failure comes in 'can'ts'.

How our thoughts lead to our behaviour

Changing the message

My thoughts. What I tell myself.	The good friend test. Would a good friend agree?	New message
You're a complete idiot to have missed that penalty.	No - my friend has seen me play well.	I'm cross that I missed that one - but I have scored more often than I've missed this season.
I'm stupid, I can't do anything.		
Everyone in the world can read except me.		
I'm always in trouble in every lesson…		
I'll go mad if I have to stay here another moment - school's so boring.		
All the teachers hate me and pick on me all the time.		
There's no point in trying - I know I can't do it.		

The helpful thought game - base-board

SUCCESS
START
EXCLUSION

The helpful thought game
- cards to make up (1)

I won't say that because I'll get sent out if I do and my dad won't take me fishing.	I won't get sent out, however hard it is to stay, because that's the target I've set myself.
I don't like her and she doesn't like me but I've sat through French before so I can do it again.	I'm probably not the only one who's finding this hard - I'll ask her to explain again.
I hate it when Jamie says that to me but I'm big enough to ignore it.	I've got a choice here, I can shut up or get a detention.
This is so boring but it will be break soon so I'll just make . a start.	The harder I'm finding this, the more satisfaction I'll get if I get it right.
I messed up that one - but that's OK - nobody's perfect.	Science may not be my best subject but I AM getting better.

The helpful thought game
- cards to make up (2)

I can only get what I want in the future by working hard now, even when it's difficult.	I'm going to give this a go for 10 minutes and see how it goes…
They can call me a keener if they want - I bet they don't when they see the car I'm going to have.	I did well on that test because I actually listened in class.
I'm not sitting next to her today - I know I'll want to chat. I'll see her at break.	They can think what they like. When I make up my mind to do something I just do it.
I can say no to my friends - if they don't respect my decisions they can't respect me much.	OK - that was stupid. But no-one will remember it in three weeks time so it's not worth going over and over it…
I didn't do well in that test because I didn't work for it - I just need to practise a bit more.	I don't know if I can do this but I'm going to have a go - it's not the end of the world if I get it wrong.

he helpful thought game
- cards to make up (3)

It doesn't make any difference if I work or not - I'll still be useless.	There's no point trying in French - she hates me anyway.
If anyone says anything to me I'll hit them - it will be their own fault.	I came bottom in that test because the teacher doesn't like me.
I'm already in trouble so there's no point going to science.	I tried in the last lesson and still came last - it's not fair.
If I do what she says my friends will say I've gone soft.	I'm only messing around because the lesson is so boring - you've got to have a bit of fun.
I've missed so many lessons there's no point trying to catch up now.	I'm going to sit with my mates whatever she says - it's the only good thing about school.

The helpful thought game
- cards to make up (4)

There's no point working - it's only school.	I will work when I'm getting paid for it - why should I work for nothing?
I just like making everyone laugh - it's more fun than sitting around writing anyway.	If she won't let me chat to my mates, I won't do her boring work.
This is the worst lesson in the world - I'm going to die of boredom.	All the teachers hate me in this school - that's why I get into trouble.
I'll think about what I want to do when I leave school.	I can't write 3 pages - it's stupid work anyway.
I only bunked off because my friends would have laughed at me if I didn't go with them.	I can hardly say no when everyone's doing it, can I?

Unit 3

Learning the Key Underlying Skills

3.1 Managing feelings

- staying in control

3.2 Getting what you want

- assertiveness skills

3.3 Having a good argument

Lesson Planning Sheet

Unit 3   **Learning the key underlying skills**

Session 1   **Managing feelings - staying in control**

Learning objectives:

▸ Identifying trigger situations

▸ Understanding and recognition of the signs that anger is building up

▸ Developing strategies for preventing anger 'taking over'

▸ Encouraging pupils not to jump to conclusions

Pupil organisation:

▸ Group discussion

▸ Individual activity

Resources needed:

▸ 1 copy per pupil of worksheets 3.1, 3.2, 3.3 and 3.4

▸ Flip-chart/whiteboard and marker

Preparation:

None.

Lesson Plan 3.1

Activity 1 - Anger: short-term benefits and long-term costs

Tell pupils that anger ('losing it') is the prime cause of behaviour that results in exclusion at secondary schools, and so it is the most important feeling to learn to control.

Everybody feels anger. It is not 'bad' to feel it - it's what we DO with it that counts.

This involves recognising our triggers, as well as the signs that anger is building up inside us, and having a range of strategies for dealing with it in ways that do not result in problems.

Ask pupils to talk about the good and bad things about getting angry, or a time they did something they regretted when angry. Note the responses on the flip-chart. After the discussion, give out **Worksheet 3.1** 'Getting angry - is it worth it?' which lists the short-term 'good' feelings, and longer-term 'costs'.

Activity 2 - Triggers

A list of triggers for anger is provided (**Worksheet 3.2**) and this can be presented in a 'fun format' by asking pupils to guess what is on it, ticking off each one that is guessed correctly. Pupils can then be given the sheet and asked to add their own 'personal' triggers.

Activity 3 - What happens when we get angry

Pupils can be asked to say what happens (inside and out) when they get angry. If the outline of a person is drawn on a flip-chart to begin with, the various suggestions can be recorded in the form of a 'diagram' with arrows pointing to the various places on the body where the reaction occurs.

For example:

- Muscles clench (especially fists)
- Face goes red or pale
- Mouth goes dry
- Pupils dilate/eyes seem bigger
- Nostrils flare
- Heart races
- Breathing becomes quicker
- Stomach churns
- Sweat
- Fidgety quick movements/restlessness

This can be explained to pupils as a primitive 'fight or flight' response.

Activity 4 - Recognising the crisis point of anger

This stage is very short, but is the 'peak' of anger. At this time the body is fully aroused and it is impossible to make any rational judgements or to understand or even listen to anything anyone is saying. It is at this stage that you are likely to do something that you will later regret.

Ask pupils:

- ▶ What does it feel like to be at the 'peak' of anger?
- ▶ What happens if a friend tries to talk to you calmly?
- ▶ What happens if a teacher threatens you with suspension?
- ▶ What might you do at this stage?

Talk about the characteristic features of the 'peak' of anger

- ▶ You will not be able to make rational judgements
- ▶ You will not be able to take someone else's point of view
- ▶ You will not be able to understand what people are saying (you may not even hear them)
- ▶ You will not care about the consequences of what you do
- ▶ All that matters at this time is getting your own way!

Pupils can be asked for examples of when they reached this point and didn't care about the consequences.

The key to managing anger is to STOP ourselves reaching crisis point.

Activity 5 - Stopping yourself from reaching the crisis point

Ask what pupils do already. Discuss times they have successfully dealt with anger and flip-chart these.

Give out **Worksheet 3.3** 'Anger blockers' and discuss which pupils use or could use.

Worksheet 3.4 illustrates a common model for blocking anger - the 'Traffic Light' model.

Activity 6 - Get the full picture

(This activity is a fun way of showing the importance of stopping and thinking before reacting, as anger is often based on a misinterpretation of the situation).

Remind pupils that it is our thoughts about situations that make us behave as we do. We often react angrily without knowing 'the full picture'. Sometimes the real situation turns out to be quite different to what we thought was happening.

Read out and discuss the examples of situations that follow. Emphasise the need for fully understanding a situation before acting. This involves stopping and thinking.

Situation 1: The spilt drink

A man pushes into you as you are carrying two pints of beer from the bar in the pub.

What do you think?

How do you feel?

You turn around to shout at him but then you notice he has a white stick and is blind/he is a friend you haven't seen for ages.

How does this change your feelings?

Situation 2 - That car cut me up

You are in a car with some friends. At the traffic lights another car comes up flashing its lights and beeping its horn. It overtakes you dangerously and forces you to swerve.

Imagine you are the boy in the first car.
Why do you think the other car has cut you up?
What are your feelings?
What do you do?

The person in the car that has cut you up is your Father. He has found your Mother unconscious at home and is speeding in order to get her to the hospital.

Were you right to be angry?
What happens to your anger when you find out 'the full picture'?

Situation 3 - The misunderstanding

You walk into a room and see your best friend on the sofa with his arm around your girlfriend.

What possible explanations are there?

What would a person with a short fuse think and do?

What might a person with a longer fuse think and do?

Activity 7 - Alternative responses to anger (pair work)

Give each pair a 'trigger situation' and ask them to come up with a range of possible responses to that situation.

Alternatively, pupils could be asked to describe a situation that has made them angry and to think about different ways to handle it.

Possible trigger situations:

- A teacher who you think does not like you shouts at you in a lesson when it is the person next to you who is talking
- Your parents refuse to let you go to a party because they are going out and want you to babysit your little sister
- A local shopkeeper accuses you of stealing from his shop (you haven't)

Pairs to feedback.

Discuss 'pros' and 'cons' of each response. Discuss 'appropriacy' of responses - over-reactions etc.

Activity 8 - Role-play: strategies in action

Pairs to chose one situation and role play it, first with an immediate impulsive response, and then using the strategies learnt.

The leader can ask participants to 'freeze' at key points, and ask the group to say what is happening in terms of each 'character's' thoughts and feelings and physiological responses.

Try to bring in:

(1st role-play)
- The trigger
- What happens to the body during the build up to the crisis point
- When the 'fight or flight' response is being activated
- Inability of angry person to listen to reason when in the crisis stage
- Action participant will probably regret (perhaps shouting abuse or hitting someone)
- What undesirable consequences might flow from angry action

(2nd role-play)
- Any attempt to avoid trigger
- Any attempt to use 'anger-blockers' or traffic-light model
- Alternative interpretations of situations
- Alternative actions to those that will result in long-term disadvantage

Hot-seating (i.e. choosing one pupil to be 'in the hot seat' in their role while others ask questions of him/her) could be used to encourage empathy with other person's feelings and recognition of the stresses that have led them to behave as they do.

Getting Angry – Is it worth it?

Good things about getting angry (short-term benefits)

▶ Feel good - sense of release

▶ Pleasure in hurting someone who has made you angry

▶ Feeling powerful

▶ Getting rid of frustration

▶ Getting what you want

▶ Admiration of friends

▶ Feeling 'tough' and in control

Bad things about getting angry (long-term costs)

▶ Going to prison

▶ Costing money - windows and computers are expensive to replace

▶ Hurting yourself or people you like (e.g. driving too fast and crashing)

▶ Feeling bad and guilty afterwards. Feeling 'out of control'

▶ People may be frightened of you and may not like you

▶ Family feeling ashamed

▶ Not getting a job because lessons have been missed through exclusions etc.

▶ Being thrown out of school

What makes me angry?

1. When people talk about me behind my back	
2. When I get my work wrong/can't do work	
3. When I'm treated unfairly	
4. When someone shouts at me	
5. When people stop me doing what I want	
6. When people call me names	
7. When people are rude about my family	
8. When someone calls me a liar	
9. When I get told off and others don't	
10. When someone pushes me	
11. When someone takes my things	
12. When there is too much noise	
13. When people won't listen to me	
14. When people laugh at me	
15. When people don't understand me	
16. When other people are angry	
17. When other people get more attention	
18. When I'm losing at football	
19.	
20.	
21.	
22.	
23.	
24.	
25.	

Anger blockers

"If you keep on doing what you're doing, you'll keep on getting what you're getting!"

1. Breath deeply - 10 times

2. Self-talk

3. Tense and relax your muscles (e.g. clench and unclench your fists)

4. Use the Turtle technique (pretend to be protected by a shell and do not respond to any provocation)

5. Walk away - move away from the situation

6. Do something different or unexpected (be charming)

7. Punch a cushion

8. Take some exercise

The traffic light model

STOP! Use anger
        Blockers.
        Get the full
        Picture.

THINK! What are my
        choices?
        Think long-term
        costs!

GO!   Do the most
        sensible
        thing.

You can't change
what other people do,
but you can change
the way things turn
out by changing
what you do!

Lesson Planning Sheet

Unit 3   **Learning the Key Underlying Skills**

Session 2   **Getting what you want - assertiveness skills**

Learning objectives:

- ▸ Developing an understanding of assertiveness and the effect of body language, eye-contact, tone of voice and choice of words
- ▸ Rehearsing assertiveness skills

Pupil organisation:

- ▸ Group discussion
- ▸ Pair activity

Resources needed:

- ▸ 1 copy of worksheet 3.5 (blown up to A3 or as an OHP if possible)
- ▸ 1 copy per pupil of worksheets 3.6, 3.7 and 3.8
- ▸ Flip-chart/whiteboard and marker
- ▸ A video recorder and playback facilities are useful, but not essential, for activity 3
- ▸ (optional) A few small prizes for activity 4

Preparation:

None.

Lesson Plan 3.2

Activity 1 - Introducing assertiveness

Explain what is meant by assertiveness - ie, saying what you mean without being aggressive (threatening or violent) or passive (accepting the situation), so that people will listen to what you say. It allows you to stay calm and in control and to get what you want without making other people angry. Ask pupils to list times that assertiveness might be useful with teachers and flip-chart the responses.

Activity 2 - What if?

The pupils discuss two or more of the following situations (in pairs):

▶ What you'd do if someone gave you a nasty note and told you had to take it to another pupil

▶ If someone grabbed your crisps/sweets ('Let me have one') without asking your permission

▶ If someone criticised your new clothes

▶ If you are supposed to be clearing up with a group and the others are leaving you to do all the work

Group discussion of what different ways of reacting there are. Teacher writes up on flip-chart.

Explain that most ways of dealing with a situation fall into one of three types of response (**Worksheet 3. 5**).

Aggressive - shouting, blaming, slagging off, making people feel small, getting your own way whatever the cost

Passive - giving in, putting yourself down, hesitating, apologising, stalling

Assertive - being honest, confident, standing up for yourself, and saying what you want without hurting other people's feelings

Explain that there are four aspects to being assertive:

▶ Body language

▶ Eye contact

▶ Tone of voice

▶ The words you use

Activity 3 - Body language

Ask the group to walk around the room as if they were the most important person in the room. Freeze group and ask for feedback on what they notice about the way they are holding themselves etc. Chart responses.

Responses might include:

> ▸ Shoulders back
>
> ▸ Head held high, nose slightly up
>
> ▸ Confident 'look'
>
> ▸ Striding walk
>
> ▸ Not looking behind
>
> ▸ Looking directly at people

Ask the group to walk around the room as if they are frightened of everybody in the room and feel like the least important person there.

Repeat freeze activity.

Responses might include:

> ▸ Shoulders hunched
>
> ▸ Head held down
>
> ▸ Unconfident 'look'
>
> ▸ Hesitant walk
>
> ▸ Looking down and behind
>
> ▸ Not looking directly at people
>
> ▸ Fiddling with hands
>
> ▸ Resting on one foot
>
> ▸ Hand movements (covering face etc)

This activity can be recorded on a video if the school has the facilities. Pupils learn a lot from watching themselves on video, as they often have no idea how they present themselves.

Emphasise that confident body language is important in making people feel confident.

Activity 4 - Eye-contact

Explain that the next task is difficult and that most groups have to have a few goes to get it right. One of the key ways of being assertive is using eye-contact. The thing to master is looking someone in the eye without letting your face show aggression and without giggling.

The task is to look each other in the eye for a full minute without giggling, smiling, or showing aggressiveness. Pupils can work in pairs, and repeat activity with a new partner. Each pair tries to hold eye-contact for 30 seconds to one minute. A few small prizes can be useful motivators.

Feedback, then repeat.

Activity 5 - Tone of voice

A third component of being assertive is using an appropriate tone of voice.

Give out **Worksheet 3.6** and explain that pupils have to say the nonsense sentence printed on it in different tones of voice.

Read the sentence and go through the different types of tone of voice listed, explaining any that aren't clear. Pupils in pairs 'say' the sentence in a particular tone of voice and their partner has to guess it. Let them have three goes each and then ask for those who scored highly to repeat their performance for the whole group.

Emphasise that how you say things influences the message received. Illustrate 'go away' said in an unassertive fashion and then in an assertive way. Encourage pupils to identify the key features of assertive language.

For example:

- ‣ Low, even voice
- ‣ Not too loud
- ‣ Clear words
- ‣ Not too fast or too slow
- ‣ Keep eye-contact

Activity 5 - Choosing your words

It is difficult to find the right words to say what you want to, especially if you are feeling angry. It can be done though, with practice, and often choosing the right words does make a difference.

The words you use can be aggressive, passive or assertive. Give out or show **Worksheet 3.7** and read out the phrases in the first example. In pairs ask pupils to mark each sentence with a 'P' if they think it is a passive thing to say, 'AG' if they think it is aggressive, and 'AS' if they think it is assertive.

When they have finished, discuss what effects each phrase might have on themselves, a friend or a teacher.

Activity 6 - Finishing the session

Ask the pupils in the group to contribute one thing that an assertive person does (eg. speaks in a low tone; stands up straight). Check how many they get against **Worksheet 3.8** 'Being assertive - a summary'.

Your choice...

Aggressive

Shouting, blaming, slagging off, making people feel small, getting your own way whatever the cost.

Passive

Giving in, putting yourself down, hesitating, apologising, stalling.

Assertive

Being honest, confident, standing up for yourself, saying what you want without hurting other people's feelings.

Being assertive - tone of voice

Say this nonsense sentence in all the different ways listed below.

'Hig, dit netter toll, nim pif nak'

Quietly   Loudly   Nervously

Crossly   Aggressively

Baby-like   High-pitched

Assertively

As if you're about to cry

Assertive, aggressive or passive?

▶ You had better…

▶ I can understand why you're annoyed, but there's no need to be so angry

▶ You'd better not be saying that I'm…

▶ Sorry, sorry, I didn't mean it…

▶ OK - let's talk about it

▶ Oi, I want a word with you!

▶ I wanted to ask you… oh don't worry… it doesn't matter

▶ You're just an idiot

▶ I'm feeling cross that you…

▶ (Just ignore it and don't say anything)

▶ I'd like you to stop doing that

▶ If you don't stop that I'm going to beat you up

▶ Oh, please don't…

▶ I'm feeling unhappy that you've asked me to stay in…

▶ I ain't staying in, so what are you going to do about it?

▶ Why is it always me that's got to stay in… it's not fair

97

Being assertive – a summary

▶ # Body Language

Shoulders back

Head held high, nose slightly up

Confident 'look'

Striding walk

Not looking behind

Looking directly at people

▶ # Eye Contact

▶ # Tone of Voice

Low, even voice

Not too loud

Clear words

Not too fast or too slow

▶ # Words to use

Say how you feel

Say what you want

Say it once

Don't threaten or plead

Lesson Planning Sheet

Unit 3   **Learning the key underlying skills**

Session 3   **Having a good argument**

Learning objectives:

▸ Recognising common causes of conflict

▸ Recognising unhelpful 'conflict behaviours'

▸ Developing more helpful behaviours for 'having a good argument'

Pupil organisation:

▸ Group discussion

▸ Pair activity

Resources needed:

▸ 1 copy of worksheet 3. 10, 3.12 (blown up to A3 or as an OHT if possible)

▸ 1 copy per pupil of worksheets 3.9, and 3. 11

▸ Flipchart/whiteboard and marker

Preparation:

(optional) Several copies of a newspaper to scan for headlines involving conflict for Activity 1.

(optional) Video clip of people having an argument to show in Activity 2.

Lesson Plan 3.3

Activity 1 - What do people argue about?

Ask pupils to list all the things they can think of that make conflict and disagreements happen at school, with teachers and other pupils, and even with friends. List their responses.

Explain that throughout life we come into conflict with others on a regular basis as individuals, members of groups and even as members of a country (eg. in war situations). To emphasise this point, pupils can be asked to look at the headlines in a daily newspaper (you will need several copies) - what examples can be found?

Activity 2 - What do people do when they are arguing?

If possible, use a film or TV clip on video to demonstrate a 'bad argument' (Eastenders is usually a good source of material).

Ask pupils to say what they, and other people, actually do when they are arguing. Write down their responses on the flipchart.

What people do when they are arguing:

examples might include...

Shouting   Threatening
Swearing   Interrupting
Insulting   Not listening
Blaming
Hitting
Trying to have the last word
Trying to make them give in
Using threatening body language
(stand close, wave fingers etc.)

Ask pupils what the effect on the other person's behaviour is when they do these things. Use examples of arguments with teachers, parents or friends. How do they feel when people do these things to them?

Ask the key question: does any of these things help solve the problem?

Activity 3 - The millionaire challenge!

Tell pupils - If you want to solve a problem (not just be horrible to someone) then there are things that you can do to have a good argument, without both of you getting very angry.

Give out or display, **Worksheet 3.9** which challenges the pupils to think of what they would have to do to prevent an argument happening with their mother or carer if there was £1 million depending on it. Talk about the problem and ask the pupils, working in pairs, to come up with five things they could do to make sure they got the money, giving prompts as necessary (eg. 'would you speak in a loud or a calm voice?'). The activity can be time-limited or presented as a competition with a small prize for the best answers.

Go through the ideas they have come up with and compare to the suggestions on **Worksheet 3.10**:

- Stopping yourself getting angry (use anger blockers)
- Not swearing or calling names
- Speaking calmly
- Using non-aggressive body-language
- Listening to the other person - letting them have a turn to speak
- Finding out WHY it matters to them
- Not using force
- Saying WHY you feel like you do
- Saying calmly what you would like to happen and why

Explain that these may seem difficult to do, and that they need a lot of practice (adults still come to blows after all), but that they do work and can be learnt.

Activity 4 - Watch the words you use

The words people use to say something can affect whether an argument gets better or worse. One thing that is guaranteed to make things worse is when people use sentences beginning with 'YOU...' Demonstrate the automatic contrary response (NO I'M NOT or YES I DO) by using a couple of examples : 'You are so lazy', 'you never finish a piece of work', 'you're always late home', 'You never do any clearing up around here'.

Ask pupils to listen to the following sentences (spoken by a teacher to a pupil) and judge which one would make them feel most angry and leave them wanting to get back at the teacher.

- You never bother bringing your book to my lesson, you make me mad...
- I feel frustrated with you when you don't bring your book to lessons because I have to stop the lesson and find paper for you, which means other people have to wait

Give out **Worksheet 3.11** (The Art of Talking to Teachers) and explain to pupils that they are to think of different ways of saying each of the statements that would be less likely to make things worse when speaking to a teacher.

Before they begin, show **Worksheet 3.12** which outlines a good rule for saying what you mean without starting an argument (the 'I-message' rule).

Ask pupils to rephrase the sentences on the worksheet using this model. The last one has been left blank for pupils' own examples. Each response could be role-played, and the likely effect on the teacher's behaviour discussed.

Activity 5 - Putting it into practice

As a follow-up, if time is available, pupils could be asked to look out for conflict situations (particularly with teachers) and to note down what happened to share with the group. The group could then discuss these, and perhaps develop short role-plays illustrating the 'best' and 'worst' ways they could be handled.

Note: The concept of using 'I-messages' comes from: Gordon, T. (1974), *Teacher Effectiveness Training*, Peter Wyden, New York

The millionaire challenge

You hear in the post that you have been offered an audition in your favourite band. The contract would be worth £1,000,000 in the first year. However, there is a problem. You desperately need your parents permission to go, and the cost of the train-fare to London. Unfortunately, as you are about to ask them, your mother comes in shouting at you because you have not done your jobs, and she is threatening to ground you!

Can you handle your mother? What would you have to do to make sure that she calms down so that you can get your dream audition? Write down five things that you would do to stop her getting any angrier…

1. _____

2. _____

3. _____

4. _____

5. _____

Ways to have a good argument

▶ Stopping yourself getting angry
(use anger blockers)

▶ Not swearing or calling names

▶ Speaking calmly

▶ Using non-aggressive body-language

▶ Listening to the other person- letting them
have their say

▶ Finding out WHY it matters to them

▶ Not using force

▶ Saying WHY you feel like you do

▶ Saying calmly what you would like to
happen and why

The art of talking to teachers

(How to do it so that you win)

Talk to make an argument happen   Talk to solve a problem

You're going too fast… how do you expect me to do the work…?	I feel_____ when you_____ because I_____
Why should I listen to you? You're so boring…	I feel_____ when you_____ because I_____
You're always picking on me, it wasn't me that wrote on the board…	I feel_____ when you_____ because I_____
(Write your own here)	I feel_____ when you_____ because I_____

Watch your words…

A good rule for saying what you mean without being mean about what you say…

Start your sentence with I, not you.	I
Say how you feel (cross, frustrated)	FEEL CROSS
Say what it is that the person is doing	WHEN YOU
	_____
Say why it makes you feel this way	BECAUSE

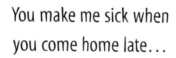

Bad Words   ## Good Words

You make me sick when you come home late…

I feel worried when you come home late because I care about you and I don't know what's happened to you…

Unit 4

Surviving Teachers and Classrooms

4.1 Rules, rights and responsibilities

4.2 The miracle lesson - A toolkit for classroom survival

4.3 Choices and consequences

- 'trigger' situations (pupil difficulties) (1)

4.4 Choices and consequences

- 'trigger' situations (responses to others' behaviour) (2)

4.5 The survival mindset

- top 10 skills

4.6 Putting it all into practice and measuring progress

Lesson Planning Sheet

Unit 4   **Surviving Teachers and Classrooms**

Session 1 **Rules, rights and responsibilities**

Learning objectives:

▸ Developing an understanding of rights, responsibilities and rules

▸ Knowing the key behavioural tasks necessary for lesson survival

▸ Identifying what pupils can do already

Pupil organisation:

▸ Group discussions

▸ Individual activity

Resources needed:

▸ 1 copy of worksheets 4.1 and 4.3 (blown up to A3 if possible)

▸ 1 copy per pupil of worksheets 4.2, 4.4, 4.5

▸ Flip chart/whiteboard and marker

▸ Glue and scissors

Preparation:

None.

Lesson Plan 4.1

Activity 1 - Identifying 'the ideal teacher'

Discuss 'what makes a good teacher?' Encourage pupils to identify the lesson they enjoy most/in which they have least problems.

Ask pupils what it is that the teacher does that helps them to enjoy/behave well in this lesson, completing the first three columns of group **Worksheet 4.1**.

If you have time, this activity can be extended to include a group or individual picture of 'the ideal teacher' with labels to indicate the key qualities identified.

Activity 2 - The nature and purpose of rules

Ask pupils what rules these teachers have in their lessons and why. Record these in the final column of **Worksheet 4.1**.

A good way of opening a discussion about rules is to ask what would happen if there were none in specific areas of life (eg. driving, football).

The basic learning point is that rules protect our basic RIGHTS within a group. Discuss with the group what rights pupils should have in school.

Key rights are:

▸ The right to feel safe
▸ The right to learn
▸ The right to be respected
▸ The right to fair treatment

Ask pupils what sort of rules we need to have in order to protect these rights. Make a list of their suggestions on the flip chart and compare their suggestions to the school rules.

Key learning points are :

▸ Rules are not there for the teacher but for all pupils
▸ With rights come responsibilities

Activity 3 - Whose responsibility?

Read out the two statements below (reproduced on **Worksheet 4.2**)

'Pupils can choose to shout, throw things around the classroom, swear, go to sleep or walk out of the classroom (and so could the teacher I guess). The teacher's job is to teach and remind pupils about the agreed rules. He or she cannot 'make them behave' - everyone's behaviour is their own responsibility.'

'The teacher should control the pupils and make them behave. That's their job.'

Which statement do pupils agree with and why? (Refer to the 'locus of control' work covered in Unit 2). In practice, while behaviour is our own responsibility, there are things teachers do that support pupils in making sensible choices (giving rewards, being clear, recognising effort etc), and these can be pointed out to pupils.

Activity 4 - The 'perfect pupil'

Ask 'what would teachers say made the perfect pupil? What would teachers see that pupil doing from the beginning of the lesson to the end?' (Prompt as necessary, eg. how would this pupil come into the classroom? How would s/he ask for help?).

Use group **Worksheet 4.3** and use it to record pupils' ideas on the qualities of the perfect pupil.

Give out **Worksheet 4.4** to pupils and compare what the pupils have come up with to the list of 'classroom survival skills' which teachers themselves have identified as the things pupils need to be able to do to do well in mainstream lessons.

Activity 5 - Self-rating

Give each pupil a copy of **Worksheet 4.5**. Ask them to rate their own behaviour (in their best lesson) on the scale of one to 10, if one is the worst pupil in the world and 10 the 'perfect pupil' discussed. Ask them what they can do already from the 'classroom survival skills checklist', (**Worksheet 4.4**) that stops them from being at 'one' (i.e. the worst pupil in the world).

Pupils can cut out the items they can already do (in their best lesson) and stick these onto the worksheet.

Our best lessons

Name	Lesson	Things the teacher does that help	Rules the teacher has

Whose responsibility?

'Pupils can choose to shout, throw things around the classroom, swear, go to sleep or walk out of the classroom (and so could the teacher, I guess). The teacher's job is to teach and to remind pupils about the agreed rules. He or she cannot 'make them behave' – everyone's behaviour is their own responsibility.'

'The teacher should control the pupils and make them behave. That's their job.'

The perfect pupil

Classroom survival skills checklist

✔ Be in the right place at the right time

✔ Line up quietly outside the classroom

✔ Walk into the classroom sensibly

✔ Sit where I'm asked to without making a fuss

✔ Remember what I need for the lesson and get my things out sensibly

✔ Listen when the teacher is talking

✔ Answer any questions I can politely

✔ Ask politely for help if I'm stuck or don't understand (not shouting out!)

✔ Put my hand up for help and WAIT if the teacher is busy
  - ▸ 30 secs
  - ▸ 1 min
  - ▸ 2 mins

✔ Have a go at the work straight away by myself

✔ Follow class rules for setting out work and keep my books neat

✔ Get on with work by myself for
  - ▸ 1 min
  - ▸ 5 mins
  - ▸ 15 mins

✔ Work sensibly in a group

✔ Stay in the room unless I have permission to leave

✔ Ask politely for permission to leave the room

✔ Stay in my seat when asked to

✔ Use 'classroom language'

✔ Treat my own and school property with respect

✔ Write down homework

✔ Pack away and leave room quietly when

Self-rating sheet

At present I rate myself a _____ on this scale (in my best lesson)

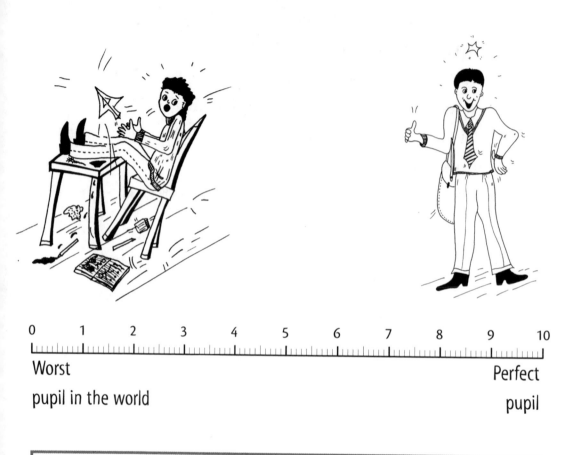

```
0      1      2      3      4      5      6      7      8      9     10
```
Worst   Perfect

pupil in the world   pupil

> I am not a '1' because I can already do these things:

Lesson Planning Sheet

Unit 4   **Surviving Teachers and Classrooms**

Session 2 **The miracle lesson - A toolkit for classroom survival**

Learning objectives:

▶ Setting goals and targets

▶ Gaining a vision of a problem-free future in school

Pupil organisation:

▶ Group discussions

▶ Individual activity

Resources needed:

▶ 1 copy per pupil of worksheets 4.6, 4.7 (enlarged to A3 if possible), 4.8, 4.9, 4.4 (from session 4.1)

▶ Plain paper (or outline of a bag or 'tool-kit'), felt pens or crayons

▶ Glue and scissors

▶ Flip chart and pens

Preparation:

None.

Lesson Plan 4.2

Activity 1- developing a picture of progress

Recap on pupil's rating sheets from previous lessons. Give out **Worksheet 4.6** and ask pupils to rate themselves (on the one to 10 scale) as to where they would like to be by the end of term/in three months. It is important to point out that they are not expected to become 'model pupils', but that if they are to be able to stay in mainstream lessons (and achieve the goals they identified in the earlier units) they will need to be able to do a lot of the things on the list. Discuss what the 'minimum' requirements might be (this will probably vary for different teachers).

Ask the pupils to identify specifically what they will be doing when they reach the point they want to get to (with reference to **Worksheet 4.4**). Another copy of **Worksheet 4.4** can be given out and items again stuck onto their copy of **Worksheet 4.6**, this time to represent what they will be able to do when they reach their target number on the rating scale.

Activity 2 - The miracle day

Ask 'If a miracle happened tonight when you went to bed, and you woke up in the morning already at your chosen point on the scale, what would be the first thing that you would notice that was different when you went into the lesson you are working on at the moment'.

Ask pupils in turn to say the next thing they would notice, then the next and so on.

Ask pupils: 'Who else would notice that the miracle had happened?

What would your friends say? What would your teacher say to another teacher in the staff room? What good things would happen because of the miracle?'

Activity 3 - Drawing the miracle lesson

Use **Worksheet 4.7** (enlarged to A3 if possible) to draw a cartoon style story about the 'miracle lesson'. Help pupils to identify and plan the main 'stages' of the story that best illustrate the miracle (eg. the pupil entering the room quietly, sitting away from disruptive friends, having correct materials etc.), and what the characters would be saying and doing.

Activity 4 - Individual target setting

Ask pupils to chose two or three things to work on from the list on **Worksheet 4.4** (those that will help them increase their scale rating) and complete **Worksheet 4.8**. Talk through the worksheet and support as necessary.

NB: The targets pupils chose will ideally be reflected on their target/report cards if these are used.

Activity 5 - Drawing the 'lesson survival kit'

Give pupils **Worksheet 4.9** 'My Classroom Survival Kit' and ask them to draw in it what they might need to help them survive in mainstream lessons. Example illustrations are given around the outside of the 'survival kit' to help pupils to grasp the idea. These include:

▸ 1 bottle of patience

▸ 1 jar of respect

▸ 1 tablespoonful of humour

▸ 1 checklist of the materials I need each day

▸ 1 packet of responsibility

▸ A script that says 'I don't like doing this but if I stick at it I'll be able to go to break on time'

Self-rating sheet

By_____ (date) I would like to be at number_____on this scale

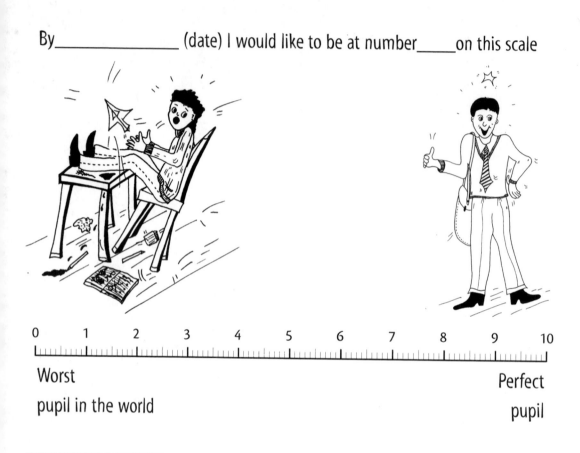

```
0    1    2    3    4    5    6    7    8    9    10
```

Worst

pupil in the world

Perfect

pupil

When I am at this number, these are the things I will be doing:

(copy or stick on sentences from worksheet 4.4).

My miracle lesson

Target setting

My targets for surviving in the classroom are:

1.

2.

3.

You will know I am working on my targets when you see me:

I will know I have achieved my targets when:

I will celebrate achieving these targets by:

The lesson survival kit

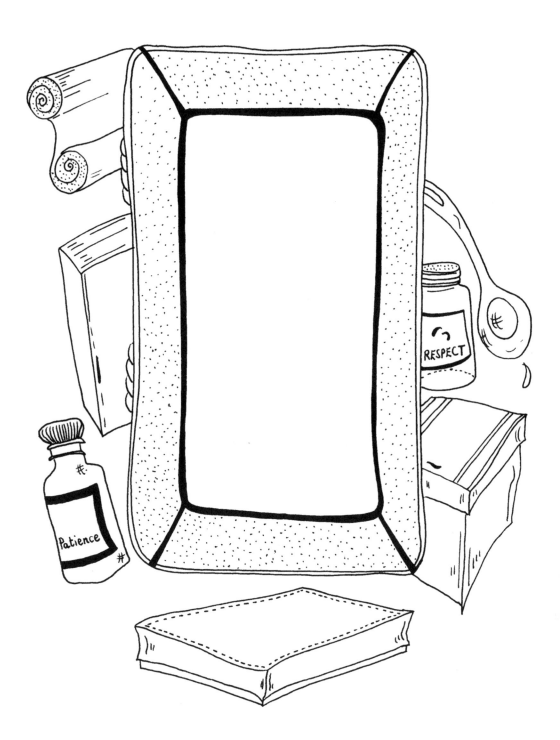

Lesson Planning Sheet

Unit 4 **Surviving Teachers and Classrooms**

Session 3 **Choices and consequences - 'trigger' situations (pupil difficulties) (1)**

Learning objectives:

▸ Identifying 'obstacles' to achieving targets and 'triggers' for poor behaviour (within pupil's control)

▸ Developing strategies for overcoming these

▸ Understanding the consequences of different behavioural choices

Pupil organisation:

▸ Group discussion

▸ Pair or small group work

Resources needed:

▸ 1 copy of worksheets 4.10 and 4.11 (enlarged to A3 if possible)

▸ Materials for making posters

▸ Video recording and playback facilities (optional)

Preparation:

None.

Lesson Plan 4.3

Activity 1 - Identifying obstacles and triggers

Recap on targets pupils have identified (on **Worksheet 4.8**). What will stop them from achieving them? Make a list of 'obstacles' - things that happen or things that teachers or other pupils do or say that 'trigger' behaviour that stops them from achieving their targets.

Divide the 'obstacles' that pupils come up with into two lists - things to do with other people (eg. friends calling out across the classroom; the teacher accusing you of something you haven't done), and things to do with the pupils themselves (eg. forgetting materials; not having done homework; having to copy too much off the blackboard; finding the work hard/boring etc.).

Explain that you will be spending the next two sessions looking at ways around these problems, starting with the things to do with the pupils themselves.

Common obstacles that pupils often raise about lessons (to do with the pupil themselves) are listed on **Worksheet 4.10**. They include:

▶ Getting into trouble for forgetting books/equipment

▶ Getting into trouble for not having done homework

▶ Not being able to do the work

▶ Not understanding what you're supposed to be doing

▶ Having to write for long periods of time

▶ Having to copy too much off the blackboard

▶ Being bored

▶ Having to say sorry to the teacher

Activity 2 - Strategies for overcoming obstacles

Select the most common obstacles raised and work on each one in turn.

For each obstacle a group/pair or individual 'What if....' poster could be made (see **Worksheet 4.11** for sample) for display or for pupils' files. This could include the particular situation in the centre and then pupils ideas on:

▶ What I can do to prevent it happening

▶ Helpful things to think

▶ Helpful things to do/say (scripts for talking to teachers etc.)

Older or respected pupils could also be 'interviewed' by the group, as to what they do in a particular situation (they may need briefing first!), and their suggestions could be included as strategies for the poster.

These activities will be useful to consolidate previous work on self-management of feelings, positive self-talk, locus of control etc.

Activity 3 - Linking action to consequence

Pupils need to understand that their behavioural choices will have different consequences (positive or negative). Each 'what if' situation should be discussed in terms of the consequences of different ways of dealing with it.

Role plays of the different situations (eg. a pupil getting told off for forgetting their equipment) could be used to explore the consequences of a negative response (getting angry with the teacher, storming out of the lesson) and a more positive one (saying sorry, saying that you will try and remember next time). They are useful for developing 'scripts' - words and phrases to use with teachers that 'work', and are often enjoyed by pupils.

If video facilities are available, it is often helpful to video the role-plays, as pupils are often surprised at how they appear to others, and useful discussion about body language and facial expressions can follow (linking into previous work on assertiveness). Although further time may need to be scheduled in to do this work, it is very useful for mainstream drama staff to be involved in these sessions, particularly those who teach the pupils in the group.

The links between the immediate consequences (detention, exclusion etc.) and the pupil's immediate and longer-term targets (discussed in earlier units) may need to be made explicit by the group leader with the key question raised each time:

'Does this result in a positive or negative outcome for YOU?'

NB: Many pupils with behavioural difficulties will take pleasure from their 'anti-authority' self-image (much of their self-esteem and peer standing may be linked to this) and they may find it difficult to apply strategies that they perceive as conflicting with this image. It is a fine balancing act to support them in maintaining their self-esteem while encouraging them to try new strategies. Many teachers have found it useful to portray the application of new strategies as the pupil 'taking charge', 'outwitting', 'handling', or even 'manipulating' the teacher through their new behaviour.

Obstacles and triggers for troublesome behaviour

▶ Getting into trouble for forgetting books/equipment

▶ Getting into trouble for not having done homework

▶ Not being able to do the work

▶ Not understanding what you're supposed to be doing

▶ Having to write for long periods of time

▶ Having to copy too much off the blackboard

▶ Being bored

▶ Having to say sorry to the teacher

WHAT IF...

I get into trouble for forgetting my stuff for the lesson

How can I stop it from happening?

▶ Have a list of what I need for each lesson

▶ Check everything is in my bag the night before

▶ Have spares at school - ask tutor/teacher to look after them

Helpful things to think if I do get into trouble

▶ Everyone makes mistakes sometimes

▶ I'll get it right next time and give Mr. X the shock of his life

▶ Don't answer back or there will be more trouble

  - it's not worth it over a pen/book

Helpful things to say if I do get into trouble

▶ Sorry - I'll remember next time

▶ Please could I borrow a pen/book as I've forgotten mine?

Who can help me?

▶ My friends can lend me stuff if I forget

▶ My tutor can check with me each morning

Lesson Planning Sheet

Unit 4 **Surviving Teachers and Classrooms**

Session 4 **Choices and consequences - 'trigger' situations (responses to others' behaviour) (2)**

Learning objectives:

▸ Identifying 'obstacles' to achieving targets and 'triggers' for poor behaviour (responses to the behaviour of others)

▸ Developing strategies for overcoming these

▸ Understanding the consequences of different behavioural choices

Pupil organisation:

▸ Group discussion

▸ Pair or small group work

Resources needed:

▸ The list of 'trigger situations' put together with pupils in previous session

▸ 1 copy of worksheet 4.12 (enlarged to A3 if possible)

▸ 1 copy of worksheet 4.11 (enlarged to A3 if possible) (from session 4.3)

▸ Materials for making posters

▸ Video recording and playback facilities (optional)

Preparation:

None.

Lesson Plan 4.4

Note: The lesson plan for lesson 4.4 follows the same format as lesson 4.3. The activities are similar and therefore the reader is asked to refer to the descriptions of activities in the preceding lesson plan, where indicated.

Activity 1 - identifying obstacles and triggers

Refer to the second list made in the previous session - the 'obstacles' identified by pupils which relate to their responses to other people. (eg. friends calling out across the classroom; the teacher accusing you of something you haven't done).

Explain that you will be spending this session looking at ways around this type of problem.

Common obstacles that pupils often raise about lessons (problems caused by the actions or behaviours of other people) are listed on **Worksheet 4.12**. They include:

- ▸ Teacher picking on you
- ▸ Teacher accusing you of doing something you haven't done
- ▸ Teacher shouting at you for something you have done
- ▸ Teacher telling you off for being late when it wasn't your fault
- ▸ Losing your temper (and ending up swearing/walking out)
- ▸ Teacher giving you a punishment that isn't fair (eg. picking up litter) and getting into a row about it
- ▸ Friends talking across the room to you and you just answering them and getting into trouble

Activity 2 - Strategies for overcoming obstacles

Select the most common obstacles raised by the group and work on each one in turn.

For each obstacle a group/pair or individual poster could be made (see **Worksheet 4.11** from the previous session for sample, and the notes on activity 2 in session 4.3).

Again, older or respected pupils could also be 'interviewed' by the group, about what they do in a particular situation (having been briefed first), and their suggestions included as strategies for the poster.

Use these activities to further consolidate previous work on self-management of feelings, positive self-talk, locus of control etc.

Activity 3 - Linking action to consequence

This provides the opportunity for further work on pupils' need to understand the consequences of their various behavioural choices, even when they perceive the situation to be 'someone else's fault'. Each 'what if' situation should be discussed in terms of the consequences of different ways of dealing with it.

Role plays of the different situations could be used (if successful in the previous session) to explore the consequences of a negative response (eg. shouting 'it wasn't me') and a more positive one (eg. using assertiveness skills). Again, scripts could be developed for dealing with these situations.

If video facilities are available, video recordings could be made and played back to pupils.

Reiterate the links between the immediate consequences (detention, exclusion etc.) and the pupil's longer-term targets (as outlined in session 4.3). Some teachers have found that a helpful question to put to pupils when dealing with behaviour that they perceive as 'someone else's fault' is 'who pays the price' - you or the teacher?'

Obstacles and triggers for troublesome behaviour (2)

▶ Friends calling out to you across the classroom

▶ Teacher picking on you

▶ Teacher accusing you of doing something you haven't done

▶ Teacher shouting at you for something you have done

▶ Teacher telling you off for being late when it wasn't your fault

▶ Losing your temper (and ending up with swearing/walking out)

▶ Teacher giving you a punishment that isn't fair (eg. picking up litter) and getting into a row about it

Lesson Planning Sheet

Unit 4   **Surviving Teachers and Classrooms**

Session 5 **The survival mindset - top 10 skills**

Learning objectives:

▸ Understanding the importance of a 'positive mind-set'

▸ Being aware of the ten key attitudinal pre-conditions of mainstream survival

▸ Identifying factors that already help them, and those that they need to develop

▸ Understanding the 'what' and 'how' of behavioural tasks necessary for a satisfactory lesson

Pupil organisation:

▸ Group discussion

▸ Pair/individual activity

Resources needed:

▸ 1 copy per pupil of worksheet 4.13, 4.14, 4.15, 4.16

▸ 1 copy of worksheet 4.4 (from session 4.1) (enlarged to A3 if possible)

▸ (optional) Video recording of 2001 film 'Castaway' and video player

Preparation:

Try to find a newspaper or magazine article about a person imprisoned in a foreign country, as this is a useful stimulus for Activity 1.

The 'model' lesson which comprises the next session will need to have been planned before this session, as the leader will be discussing it with the group in this session in order to prepare them.

Lesson Plan 4.5

Activity 1 - Survival thoughts

Introduce the idea of 'survival thoughts'. To survive anywhere you must think in a way that will help you to survive. Use the example of a man imprisoned for a long time in a foreign country (newspaper reports are a good stimulating source of 'real' information about imprisonment).

The recent film 'Castaway' provides a wonderful stimulus for this activity. If it is possible to hire a video of the film, play it from when the plane begins to crash to the point at which the hero stands on the beach exhausted and staring out to sea. (Teachers are advised to view the film section prior to playing it in order to ensure that the language used is acceptable to the school, and if it is felt to be too 'strong' to ensure parental permission is granted to view it).

What thoughts would enable someone to behave in a way that would mean they could survive in dire circumstances? Use **Worksheet 4.13** to separate the thoughts into those that would help someone survive and those that would not. Pupils could work in pairs with a joint product expected at the end.

Remind pupils of previous work on the links between thoughts, feelings and behaviour. Tell pupils that there are 10 key 'survival thoughts' that will help them to succeed in class and achieve their goals. Ask them if they can guess what they might be.

Activity 2 - My own survival thoughts

Compare their responses with **Worksheet 4.14**. Refer back to work covered in the programme (eg. having a long-term vision, positive messages about their ability to achieve their goals, peer pressure, handling 'trigger situations', work on rules and responsibilities etc.).

Give each pupil a copy of **Worksheet 4.15** and ask them to join those 'survival skills' that they already know they have to the picture with an unbroken line. Then ask them to join those that they have 'sometimes' to the picture with a dotted line. Those that they do not have at all are not yet joined to the picture.

At the end of the course, or at review meetings, their pictures can be reviewed and any changes in attitudes or thoughts recorded.

Activity 3 - Planning the 'ideal lesson'

Explain that the next session will be a 'practice' session, to see how well the pupils are able to keep to the targets they have set themselves, with a member of staff observing.

Recap on the checklist of tasks (**Worksheet 4.4**, from session 4.1) and show pupils **Worksheet 4.16**, which covers the same skills but as a checklist for a teacher observing pupils in a lesson. Explain that their observer will be completing the check-list for each of them.

Ideally pupils would be able to choose who their 'observer' would be - perhaps a senior manager who could be invited to watch their 'ideal lesson'.

The content of the lesson (which can be anything at all, but should approximate to a standard subject lesson) could be explained at this time and the expectations made very clear, using the checklist as a guide. Key behaviours could be modelled or role-played at this point.

Lesson Planning Sheet

Unit 4   **Surviving Teachers and Classrooms**

Session 6   **Putting it all into practice and measuring progress**

Learning objectives:

▸ Practising skills and tasks in supported 'model lesson'

▸ Assessment of progress in behaviour change and confidence

Pupil organisation:

▸ As demanded by teacher's individual lesson plan

Resources needed:

▸ A copy of worksheet 4.16 for observer (from session 4.5)

▸ As demanded by teacher's individual lesson plan

▸ 1 copy per pupil of worksheet 4.17

▸ (optional) Certificates and rewards for each pupil

Preparation:

The observing teacher will need to be fully briefed before the session.

Lesson Plan 4.6

Activity 1 - The model lesson

The 'ideal' lesson discussed with pupils at the last session is delivered by the leader of the group during this session. The content should reflect the type of tasks generally set in lessons and, in order to enhance the chances of pupils being successful, the lesson will need to reflect 'best practice' with motivating subject matter, tasks matched to pupils' abilities and attention spans etc.

The role of the observer (who should have been briefed beforehand) is to complete the checklist (**Worksheet 4.16**) for each pupil (up to five pupils names can be added to the checklist) and give positive feedback at the end of the session.

Activity 2 - Debriefing and assessment

15 minutes should be allowed at the end of the lesson for positive feedback to be given to the pupils, who can share with the observer the targets they are currently working on.

Worksheet 4.17 should then be completed by pupils. This asks them to rate their current behaviour on a scale of one to 10, their wish to improve their behaviour, and their confidence that they can do so. These ratings can then be compared with the ratings they gave themselves at the beginning of the programme (recorded on **Worksheet 1.1** - completed in the initial session). Certificates and rewards could be given out at this time.

NB: If pupils have had a bad lesson or are upset for any reason, do not undertake the rating exercise, but arrange to complete it with the pupil when they are feeling calm, in a one to one situation.

Suggested follow up

A model for the reintegration of pupils into mainstream lessons is outlined in the introduction, 'Reintegration and follow up'.

Survival thoughts

Imagine you have been arrested in a foreign country and put in prison for something you didn't do. Which thoughts would help you to behave in a way that would ensure that you survive and do sensible things to try to get out? And which would be unhelpful?

▶ I can't stand this a moment longer

▶ I'll just concentrate on getting through today

▶ No-one is ever going to get me out of here

▶ There's no point even writing to my family - I'll probably never see them again anyway

▶ I'm so miserable - I don't really care if I never get out

▶ I survived yesterday, so I can survive today

▶ It's not fair

▶ I know I've got a good future... I'm getting better at being patient now

▶ It's lucky I'm a strong person - others might not survive this

Top 10 survival thoughts for making it through school!

My life will be better if I can be in the classroom

I want to improve my behaviour

I believe that I can improve my behaviour

I accept that I am in charge of my own behaviour

I can talk about what's gone well and what's gone wrong

I know that it's up to me to say sorry when I'm in the wrong

I know why rules are there and I accept that (mostly) they're fair

I am strong enough to ignore the opinions of unhelpful friends

I accept that the teacher will not always 'get it right' and deal with it

I know what to do if there's a problem, and I can handle it

I will survive…

Classroom survival skills observation checklist

Name: Lesson:

CLASSROOM TASKS				
Is in the right place at the right time in uniform				
Lines up quietly outside the classroom				
Walks into the classroom sensibly				
Sits where asked without making a fuss				
Remembers materials for lesson and gets out sensibly				
Listens when the teacher is talking				
Answers register/ questions				
Asks politely for help when stuck or doesn't understand (does not shout out)				
Puts up hand for help and waits for 30 seconds, 1 minute, 2 minutes				
Has a go at work straight away (within 1 min) independently				
Follows class rules for setting out work and keeps book neat				
Focuses on independent work for 1 min, 5 mins, 15 mins				
Works well in a group				
Stays in room unless has permission to leave				
Asks politely for permission to leave the room				
Stays in seat when asked to				
Uses appropriate 'classroom language' (ie. not rude, no swearing)				
Treats own and school property with respect				
Writes down homework				
Packs away and leaves quietly				

Progress assessment

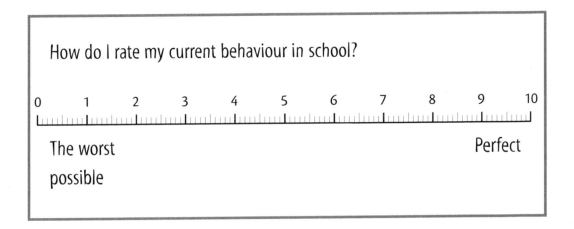

How do I rate my current behaviour in school?

| 0 | 1 | 2 | 3 | 4 | 5 | 6 | 7 | 8 | 9 | 10 |

The worst
possible

Perfect

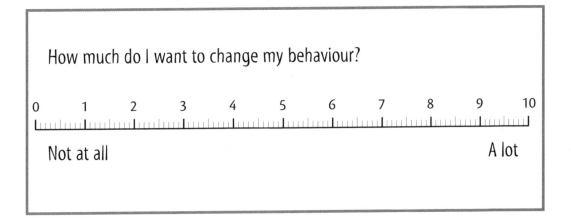

How much do I want to change my behaviour?

| 0 | 1 | 2 | 3 | 4 | 5 | 6 | 7 | 8 | 9 | 10 |

Not at all

A lot

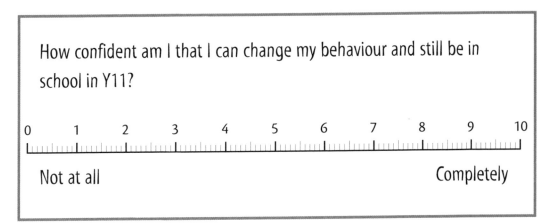

How confident am I that I can change my behaviour and still be in school in Y11?

| 0 | 1 | 2 | 3 | 4 | 5 | 6 | 7 | 8 | 9 | 10 |

Not at all

Completely

Bibliography

Bates, J. (1999) Retracking - *A photocopiable resource pack aimed at promoting student effectiveness*, South Devon Psychology Service.

Faupel, A. Herrick, E. and Sharp, P. (1998) *Anger Management. A Practical Guide*, David Fulton Publishers.

Gordon, T. (1974) *Teacher Effectiveness Training*, Peter Wyden New York.

Maines, B. and Robinson, G. (1999) *You can... you know you can (a self-concept approach)*, Lucky Duck Publishing.

McSherry, J. (1999) *A reintegration checklist*, Senjit.

Rhodes, J. and Ajmal, Y. (1995) *Solution focused thinking in schools*, BT Press.

Walters, D. and Barlow, J. (2000) *The behavioural curriculum. A whole school approach to teaching positive behaviour and emotional competence in the primary school*, Cumbria County Psychology Service.

Wardle, C. (2002) *School Survival*, Lucky Duck Publishing.

White, M. (1999) *Picture This. Guided Imagery for Circle Time*, Lucky Duck Publishing.